OVERCOMING OUR OBSESSIONS

A Spiritual Odyssey

by Philip Ferranti

with Anne Hardy

An ETC Publication

Library of Congress Cataloging in Publication Data

Ferranti, Philip, 1945-
Overcoming our obsessions.
1. Spiritual life. 2. Obsessive-compulsive neuroses.
I. Title.
BV4501.2.F453 248'.86 78-31663
ISBN 0-88280-069-8

Published by ETC Publications
Palm Springs
California 92263

Printed in the United States of America

CONTENTS

Dedication

This book is gratefully dedicated to all those concerned and loving friends who shared themselves and their love with me. Especially am I thankful to Anne and Sam Hardy and all the young people at Turn-Off, Incorporated who shared with me the realities of this book. There were hugs, kisses, tears, jokes, frustrations, hopes and fears . . . experiences. Through all these there remained a spirit of love a Presence of God.

In Appreciation,
Philip Ferranti

San Francisco

The Twelve Steps of Alcoholics Anonymous

1—We admitted we were powerless over alcohol—that our lives had become unmanageable

2—Came to believe that a Power greater than ourselves could restore us to sanity.

3—Made a decision to turn our will and our lives over to the care of God *as we understood Him.*

4—Made a searching and fearless moral inventory of ourselves.

5—Admitted to God, to ourselves and to another human being the exact nature of our wrongs.

6—Were entirely ready to have God remove all these defects of character.

7—Humbly asked Him to remove our shortcomings.

8—Made a list of all persons we had harmed, and became willing to make amends to them all.

9—Made direct amends to such people wherever possible, except when to do so would injure them or others.

10—Continued to take personal inventory and when we were strong promptly admitted it.

11—Sought through prayer and meditation to improve our conscious contact with God, *as we understand Him,* praying only for knowledge of His will for us and the power to carry that out.

12—Having had a spiritual awakening as the result of these steps, we tried to carry this message to alcoholics, and to practice these principles in all our affairs.

Introduction

From my point of view I've observed that every human is in a process that goes beyond changes in our external environments, the world which we create and place ourselves into where we live out the play of our lives. There are goings on within. There are emotions, ideas being dealt with, and even a person, a spirit or self that some of us discover. At one end of the spectrum people are really in a plight, unhappy and depressed, unproductive in their lives. A key concern here are obsessions which control the individual to the extent that their life becomes a battle ground where the person is not "living", he is rather "being lived" by his obsessions . A flow of energy, self, and love within himself, and between other human beings is non-existant or too weak to effect positive changes. An obsession as defined in this book is an irresistible preoccupation with a fixed idea or unwanted feeling. Most of us know directly or indirectly the pain and chaos of such extreme obsessions as alcoholism, drug abuse; but even minor ones can contain our growth as a person and restrict our capability to function with a sense of well being. These obsessions, depending on the extent of their grip on the individual, are things like gambling, overeating, smoking, that often prove devastating.

In a society where obsessions are often the rule of human behavior, certain values and attitudes we meet everyday have had the effect of creating the feeling and idea that there are healthy obsessions that we can cater to and it's alright to get as many of these "serviced" as our little hearts desire. Power, control, dominance and outright aggression over people, things and events in our lives, "them" whoever "they" are, and even our very life is o.k. Look out for number one, first, last always. The people in this space are wearing their guns loaded on the defensive, manipulating people and situations to a satisfactory outcome for themselves, and really don't give two hoots and a holler about who they step on or how much it hurts. And too often our society says, "that's o.k. Survival of the fittest."

Now there is another "obsession" or "rift" in the human fabric that so many of us are burdened with and involved in. This is the obsession of human relationships, with a "someone" out there, and most often we are talking about male-female involvement, is going to make things alright within, cover up the hurt, divert me from myself, and all that unfinished business of coming to a workable, fullfilling confrontation with my life. The theme song here is sex, dependency and domination. I've heard a long and endless "line" of people sharing with me the pain, chaos and suffering, even helplessness which relationship obsessions, people and emotion obsession, going from this person to the next, creates in their lives. If only they could find the key to leaving this merry-go-round.

This book, I trust, provides a path, a way to go, for all degrees of obsessions. Yet it goes further. Many of us wish to expand from an already good base of operations our lives have become. The program we discuss will fit the bill and then some. The "path" we will see unveiled is for all of us "just folks." It requires, as we shall see, a desire to change, to grow and expand ourselves in a joyful, happy, meaningful way. We will learn something of surrender, the process of giving up and disattaching ourselves from those painful thorns in our sides, obsessions. Yet with obsessions lessening and leaving our consciousness, we will find too a release from that constant flow of ideas, a mind-structure of voices, judgements, concepts, prejudices, erroneous beliefs and our cataloging and categorizing people into race, looks, sex appeal, money, status, intelligence . . . "them." Emotions and our addiction to them will lessen in their undesirable power over us . . . if we so choose, and work the program we will prevail. To change we must want to change, we must act, and see the responsibility we have in the creation of and attachment to the unwanted clutter of certain ideas, feelings, desires, obsessions in our life.

As the book unfolds we'll discuss various obsessions and the underlying cause of ego centeredness. Then we'll embark on a journey through the spiritual life, our basic "fertilizer." Each step follows in order of application but in real life, most of us learn one here, one there and seek to make things whole in our search to bridge the gaps and fill the empty spaces between various "steps" and principles of the "program." Sometimes it really does come together in our discovery and application of the missing links.

In short, we must confront a basic proposition, "Do I want to be happy, be myself or don't I?," and "If I do, do I want to do all that I have to do to get there?" From here, it's always "up" . . . to us.

"Up" can come to mean a real peace in our lives as they really unfold in a personal way, from our center of "self," and not our isolating, defensive, separatist, controlling, self-willed "ego." Our lives are then just lived out, like the flower coming to bloom, a part of the greater Life in and around us.

With this possibility in mind, take this book to heart, and enjoy the fruits of "your" labor.

One

THE WORKING OUT OF OUR LIVES

At any time during my twenties, had anyone asked me, "Is your life working out for you?" my answer would have been a fast "No!" And during this same decade I had the opportunity to travel, both in this country and abroad, and saw with most people I met a similar situation of "unworking" lives.

And what about you, my reader, is your life coming together, at its heart, in those places that are deepest and where it really counts? Let this exchange between us be a real sharing, even though I won't be able to hear your responses. That you hear your own, really hear and listen to the inner workings of your true self—that's good enough for me.

And yes, I've known a few people and places. Took work as a ranch foreman, grape-picker, fruit packer, truck loader, printer, hospital orderly, ranch hand, cab driver, bartender, bell hop, waiter, bus boy, paid people unemployment, teacher, counselor, therapist, writer . . . and through this rich contact with people came to recognize some painful themes working their way through and around people's lives.

Many of us have forgotten how to smile, to laugh quickly and freely; we too often cannot make the simplest of commitments, telling someone we're going to do such and such with them and fail to do so; or that we'll be here or there at a certain time, and aren't. At times we'll walk right by an ice cream shop and fail to go in and treat ourselves to that favorite flavor of ours. A sunny day outside and we don't leave the cares behind and walk out into it, over to a lush green park waiting nearby to help us forget this urban sprawl.

When was the last time we enjoyed the sunrise or quietly gazed upon a sunset? What about our friends, those very special ones who accept everything about us, allowing us to enjoy our own brand of craziness with them., with whom its like being snuggled, two bugs in a rug on some winter day? Peaceful moments, quiet, noise and chatter non-existent, times to ourselves and with our God. And I must not forget "playing," because that really is deficient in our day-to-day living. Many of us don't, can't, have forgotten how, never knew how to really play.

Certainly this list of absences can be extended. Perhaps I've already overdone it. But the fact remains from my own experiences telling me that too often I, you, we, failed to, well, to LIVE. And I'm not interested in another kind of list that would read, "When is the last time you drank good bourbon, went to Europe, bought a Porsche, scored with a beautiful girl, was recognized as a celebrity, a number one in something, of being the fox you think you are, winning big at Las Vegas, saw the latest movie or the TV program with the highest ratings, or read the latest best seller . . ." and I don't think, deep down, that you really are interested either. Life is not what society around us holds up for us to imitate, spend the bucks to pursue and win.

Life is real, here-and-now, what's right in front of our faces real; what we can touch, hold and be held by, smell and caress, smile at, laugh over, cry about, offer a small yet total "thank you" to someone somewhere, run and swirl and kick up our heels about. Life is people, and that ever changing, vital flow of feelings, concerns, sharings, acceptances and belongings, understandings and longings, farewells and hello's.

Yet, there were so many times, so many long unbounded timeless spaces in my life where life didn't exist at all. When just to be touched by another human being, a caring caress would have been enough. Emptiness, a hollow sounding, for-whom-the-bell-tolls kind of stillness. The wide open spaces of the far West couldn't compare. Have we shared together in this, you lonely trucker on your long haul, customers at my bar, you teenagers, young people who let me know just how much it did hurt inside; you my farm laborer friend up from Old Mexico away from family and friends, stranger-in-a-strange-land; and my housewife students; lonely even when your husbands are there and a babe is in your arms . . . all of us, a little empty, searching for a promised peace, a promised land.

As for myself for many years I was like Moses. Not only wandering the Sinai Desert (thank God it *wasn't* for forty years) of my own life, but meeting people who seemingly had found home. And all I could do was look across the "River Jordan" at the happiness these folks had fashioned for themselves . . . marriages that really were founded in love and friendship, families that really could play together, people who were *real,* who walked like they talked, knew they were plugged in somewhere to a source of love and light that did make a difference in their lives.

During my sojourn in my own "desert" I used many ways to try and get out. These paths and directions never really went anywhere but rather took me to places of pain and frustration. Loneliness and anxiety I came to know as *obsessions.*

An obsession is an irresistible preoccupation with a fixed idea or unwanted feeling. The underlying obsession that for me drove my life hither and yon was the belief that being in love, having the whole packaged deal with a woman to love, sex, romance, marriage was going to do it; it was going to produce instant happiness and cure this aching inside. Actually this was not so much the presence of suffering, although I had my share, as it was the feeling of something missing, a whole big emptiness that had to be filled up.

There were other obsessions that I allowed to take my life into their hands. once I discovered sex . . . well it *is* fun, to a point. And gambling in the form of the stock market; and that was a good one for me because it allowed me the prideful illusion that I really did know Wall Street, that I could really play that game with the Big Boys. Had to get a college degree, had to. Don't stop at a B.A., get your Master's Degree, shoot for a PhD—but I was out of ammunition by that time. And on I could go; sound familiar? We really *do* have something in common then, this being human and seeking human solutions to what's eating away at us.

All over this country we are reading road maps, following our obsessions in the hopes of finding a lasting peace, our longed for happiness. We're making our faces and bodies appealing for each other, filling up our bank accounts, garages, gas tanks, bellies; we're playing it cool, trying to protect the image that we're on the right path, we've got it together, are reading the 'right' map. Others can let us know how successful we are, how important, how ultimately necessary, how beautiful we are. Worship at our altar because we're heading for the promised land in style, even know the latest dances when we get there. And not just in this country, but a whole lot of other places and people are reading the same map, living out the same obsessions.

Does it work? Are our maps correct and our happiness assured; our true self, is it within reach? The statistics? 15,000,000 American alcoholics; 20,000,000 with recognized mental illness (conservative estimate); a near 50 percent divorce rate; etc. Forget the statistics. Just take a careful look at our world, our neighborhood, the people we meet everyday because this is our world, where we are touched by people and given the opportunity to touch in return. Society, that undefined sprawl for which there can be no dialogue, the unresolved, nebulous "they," . . . that society we can forget. But in our lives, do our answers work? Or are they fancy names, a cover-up for our obsessions?

At this point you need to know where I'm coming from, share in some of my experiences, background . . . even friends. For several years I've worked as a teacher-counselor at a teenage recovery house for alcoholics, drug users. Actually, we could have called our ranch "The House of the Obsessed." The young people who come there have just about everything going for them in the way of obsessions that you could ask for: sex, alcohol, drugs, food, gambling, etc. But during the time they are at this house, *Turn-Off, Inc.,* they get better. Slowly, one-by-one, they begin releasing their obsessions, quit reading those false maps of theirs, and start heading for their real "home," self-realization.

The director of *Turn-Off,* Anne, one of the live-in counselors, house mothers if you will, Andrea, and I chewed the fat a lot . . . dialogued, shared, talked. You're invited in to listen throughout the remainder of this book; not so much their words, but certainly their lives taught me something. I did learn . . . and for me, that wasn't easy!

ANNE: It's that something out there to make it right again, something to fill up the emptiness inside which obsessive compulsive people have. They call it different things but it's an emptiness inside. I once heard a psychiatrist discussing the obsessive compulsive. His statement was there is no cure for an obsession; there is no cure for it psychiatrically or medically. We can arrest it for a while with sex, drugs, alcohol, overwork sometimes, food, gambling, whatever it is. But the only way, in his statement, was "there is no cure for an obsession, therefore the answer must be spiritual." There are people who find relief from obsessions and compulsions for a short period of time using other methods of trading compulsions. Getting off drugs and alcohol and becoming sexually obsessive, getting off all three and becoming over-eaters, getting off all four and becoming gamblers, whatever. But the people who arrest that obsession and compulsion are people who over the long haul find a spiritual experience. And they are the only ones I've heard who do.

PHILIP: What do teenagers get into prior to drugs and alcohol as an obsession? Obviously, not gambling, because they are not going to go to Las Vegas.

ANNE: The feeling that is a common denominator of all obsessive compulsive people is the hunger and an inner restlessness for something. The teenager that doesn't fill that up with self-destructive kinds of things like alcohol, sex, whatever, many times will be obsessively social in school and athletics. These are called healthy ways of filling up that whole. But I think we all have that hunger. I think human beings have it. I think it's existential, almost.

PHILIP: The way I see it is that if the ego is central to the consciousness, then the ego becomes its own self-sustaining existence, its own satisfaction. When the self is placed at the center, the self realizes that it is perfect already. It need not do anything to find peace.

ANNE: And what teenager knows that?

PHILIP: Well, most human beings are not to the point of coming close to that. But this I think is very basically seen as the process. If you can imagine two concentric circles, one of the ego and one of the self, and they are overlapping in places; the places where the self is totally excluded you have obsessive-compulsive behavior and addiction. The place in the center where you have overlapping ego and self you have somewhat of a healthy personality, but they are also engaged in some obsessions for a while. Knowing you are your self, you have total peace. But there comes a need to balance the two. I have seen an awful lot of stress from an adult society for values which are totally ego oriented like success, security, achievement. status, power, money. Our society produces ego-oriented people.

ANNE: I also believe there are certain common denominators to all obsessive-compulsive people and that thing you were just talking about is part of what causes that person to become that type of person. Certainly, not everyone is an obsessive-compulsive person. I have found one thing among all obsessive-compulsive people. Every obsessive-compulsive personality I have ever met and talked with at any length, any depth at all, has said that the love they were given by their parents was contingent upon their performance and withdrawn when the performance didn't measure up. The kind of love that my family gave to each other and to their children was always contingent on their performance and withdrawn when the performance didn't measure up. They had certain standards that no one, no child, could live up to. "If you love me, you wouldn't do that." Love was always a weapon and it was a trap. Before I had enough experience and education to put the thoughts into words, I used to wonder why they didn't just love me like I was. What was wrong with me? And that's the feeling most of these types of personality have. How come you can't love me just because I am? And we very rarely, until much later in life, put that into words in our own mind. But that's the feeling; what's wrong with me? Why am I different? I do not know if that is in the obsessive-compulsive person, or if it is the kind of love that is given to them by their parents. I know this: I have a sister who was a love child. I was not a child of a love union, my mother had me when she didn't want me by a man she didn't love. My sister, who was raised in the same household that I was, was the child of my step-father and my mother who were very much in love. They wanted her, they planned her, they wanted her, and they loved her. My sister was raised in much the same environment that I was, and yet my sister has a basic sense of her own value. If you would ask her today did you feel love, she would say "always." "No matter what Mommy and Daddy did, I knew they always loved me." I never knew that. I always knew they did not. Now whether that was my interpretation or their lack of love I'll probably never know because they would never say. But I find that I am not unusual at all.

PHILIP: Well, then in the actual living of life what might happen is that the person fails to feel the sense of self, not only self worth but "self" itself. Not having that, they are given over to their ego which is totally performance oriented and now the problem becomes, what can I do, what must I do, what must I perform, not only for the parent, but for society around me? Not only for society but for the institutions in society, like organized religion. If you go to church every Sunday, you are a nice person. Always performance oriented. So you latch on to that ego and what it must do. Or judged, are your feelings being judged?

ANDREA: Yeah, my feelings were always labeled. That's a ridiculous way to feel. There is no such word as mad. There is no such word as hate. Why do you feel that way? What are you afraid of? Finally one day I shut up. I just stopped. It was over; I couldn't put myself in that position again. I felt like a long nerve which they had stomped on long enough. I was no longer going to let it happen. I don't know if it's true for everbody. I was a very sensitive kid and that sounds like "poor me." But I was. That's that. I didn't know how to deal with those sensitivities. I didn't feel I was given anything to cope with them. There were no guidelines. I watched my mother go bezerk and cry and throw and break things. So I did it; I figured that's one way. My mom did it and my brother did it, my sister did it. That's the way we lived. I came out and found out a whole bunch of people didn't do that. So my defenses came up and what covered the fear and inadequacies was hate and anger. That wasn't acceptable either. I found as a child that if I was really good and happy, I was ignored. So I went the opposite way to get attention. That's not to say that my mom didn't try. She did with everything she had and she didn't have much to deal with. I've heard my mother's story and it reads like a dying novel, the crap that lady went through. But it wasn't until I was a lot older that I knew that, and I saw my own selfishness as a child. I wasn't given any tools to cope with anything.

PHILIP: So taking this whole compositive of parental reactions to you, of feelings of inadequacy, of pent up anger and frustration, fear, carrying this over into high school and being a teenager and finally into adulthood and doing things which you really didn't want to do but you were programmed, you felt this was the right way to go, and all during this time you were, at least part of the time, you were using either drugs or alcohol?

ANDREA: Yeah, either drugs or alcohol or food to make it better.

PHILIP: How old were you when you got to the point of beginning to do something about this problem?

ANDREA: I was 25 years old. I had a suicide attempt. I just wanted to be left alone and I wanted to go to sleep for a while.

PHILIP: You wanted to stray from those feelings?

ANDREA: Yeah, because nothing was worth it anymore. Nothing had worked. I had been going to a marriage counselor for a year and that didn't work. My whole thing as an addict and alcoholic was that the world had to change 'cause I couldn't. The man I was married to in no way could see that he had anything wrong with him. I had to look at me and the thing was brought up to me by the marriage counselor and I couldn't face it . . . so I went home.

PHILIP: Face the feelings that you had to change?

ANDREA: Yeah, I had been molested for four years by my step-dad. He said why? You must have enjoyed it if you let it go on for that long. Who do you tell that to as kid between the ages of 8 and 11 when it was going on? I got the attention, but my mind knew it was wrong. I didn't understand that we were born with sexual feelings. I'd never been told that. I was never told that sex was dirty, but in actions I was told they were. There was a contradiction in there all the time. There seemed to be contradictions all my life. I lived with the feelings of being dirty because part of me enjoyed it but my mind was telling me what a rotten little girl I was. When the psychiatrist brought that up to me, I couldn't face it. I couldn't touch my body and the only thing I knew was that I had to get out. No amount of drugs could get rid of that feeling. I had three children and couldn't get drunk because I was afraid one of them might die. I had been told that if I didn't love my kids, they would die. There wasn't anything to give them. I didn't have any love to give them because I was depending on me and there wasn't anything in me. It was all society's opinions and all my mother's opinions and everyone else's opinions. I'd never had any of my own.

PHILIP: In other words, you never really asserted who you were?

ANDREA: Yeah, I didn't know who I was. I just didn't.

PHILIP: So at this point you avoided suicide but at the same time you came to something that turned your whole life around?

ANDREA: When I got out of the hospital I sat on the floor for three days and I didn't do anything. I tried to get my spirit to leave my body. I knew that I could do it. Just before it left, something inside me wouldn't let me die. The thing occurred to me, if my body stops, my mind will continue to run and I will live in that quiet desperation of insanity.

PHILIP: If you will talk about the whole idea of running, what does that really mean? Not only when teenagers come to Turn-Off Incorporated, but people in general.

ANDREA: For me running was done all in my head. I didn't do the geographic running. They talk about alcoholics doing geographics, moving from town to town. But when I was drinking and using, I ran emotionally. I ran fantasy. I didn't like being what I was or doing what I was so anything was better. I lived totally within a fantasy world. I could do that because I had control over my fantasies.

PHILIP: Do you find that that is one of the characteristics of an alcoholic or an obsessive personality, a lot of fantasy?

ANDREA: Yeah, self-deception and self-delusions. Somewhere I even lost control of my fantasies because they destroyed me. They would start out really neat and after that self punishment they were really coming out bad. They would end up in tragedy or death . . . and I'm miserable again. I escaped in TV for a long, long time because that was better than what I had gone through myself. A lot of alcoholics will move physically from town to town thinking it will be different this time. That's really dumb because you are still going on the same ideas, the same concepts you had in the other town and it isn't going to change.

PHILIP: Do you find there is a large percentage of alcoholics that use this geographical moving, this migratory, gypsy-like attitude to solve problems?

ANDREA: Most of them talk about the geographics and for a long time I felt like I didn't belong because I didn't do those things.

PHILIP: When you say that, it's incredible because we have always been distinguished, in at least the last 20 years, as a mobile society in our country. One out of four Americans move every year. I wonder if that has a direct correlation to the fact that alcoholism and the obsessive alcoholic personality is so widespread in society that what we are really seeing is a form of adjustment.

ANDREA: Yeah, I think so. The only thing that keeps me coming through is that it's going to be different this time. I hear normal people saying that and I don't really look at the world as normal. I see them all as alcoholics. Some are workoholics, some beat their kids. Everbody does something excessively to escape. And it's going to be different this time.

PHILIP: To escape what?

ANDREA: Reality and themselves. Something out there is going to make it better in here.

PHILIP: What is so bad inside?

ANDREA: My concept of myself is that I couldn't live with my thoughts because I was told they were no-no's. After all, all my life I'd been told my thoughts were wrong. I wasn't supposed to have them.

PHILIP: You couldn't remember your feelings either?

ANDREA: No. I couldn't get in touch with my feelings because they were wrong too. I didn't have to deal with them. I couldn't express them to anybody. That had been proven many, many times in my life. I talked to so-called normal women who had children. They say that they love them then they push them around and reject them. They couldn't stand them, but they wouldn't dare say that right at the moment they can't stand their kids. That's a no-no. Society tells you that is an absolutely terrible thing to say, that you have rotten kids and can't stand them. I watched a lady who had babies on a regular basis, ten of them for God's sakes, and she still wasn't happy. The only time she was happy was when she was pregnant. She was obsessive in having babies and she couldn't stand any of the ones she had. She used to beat them. She couldn't openly admit and say she couldn't stand these kids. While I'm pregnant it's nice because everyone loves a pregnant woman. After the baby is born comes the responsibility.

PHILIP: So you think most obsessive people are running in society?

ANDREA: Yes I do. They are running from themselves and reality and responsibility. The whole shot. It gets back to the thing that we just said, that I am all there is. There isn't anything else.

PHILIP: And people don't want to accept the responsibility of them doing it. In terms of accepting it at gut level, what do you think people have to do in order to get there. As you say, some of the kids sometimes don't really hit bottom. What kind of a bottom do they hit?

ANDREA: I think the kids that come here are forced to look at it because a lot of them are back in juvenile hall or jail. One of the requirements to come to Turn-Off is that you want help. They are faced with juvenile hall. Rather than going to juvenile hall or some other such place, Turn-Off sounds kind of groovy. There's no locked gates, there is no lock-up for them. They come in figuring they can con everybody. Usually in about thirty days is when the changeover hits. I don't honestly know why this is. It took me three years of thinking things over before I reached an emotional gut level. Inside the innermost self I knew I was an alcoholic, a real alcoholic, not so much in drugs but in the alcohol part of it. Whether that is part of my insanity and my alcoholism, the -ism part of it, or what it was, but I was three years on the program before to my innermost self I accepted the fact that I was a real alcoholic. Before that, whenever I said I was an alcoholic, my head clicked off "potential." And that was enough to keep me in A.A. But I didn't come into A.A. to stop drinking. I came in to stop my mind.

PHILIP: Are you saying that just in the everyday process of living you had a flow of thoughts in your mind that just wouldn't stop and you were being mentally harrassed by ideas?

ANDREA: Yes. It went 24 hours a day when I wasn't sleeping and I couldn't shut it off at any point. That's why I used drugs and alcohol.

PHILIP: Do you think a lot of people have that kind of flow of consciousness that they can't control?

ANDREA: The people that I've talked to and heard, yeah, they have those three little voices in their heads, sometimes more.

PHILIP: The three little voices?

ANDREA: You refer to it as the parent-child and the adult and that is what I'm aware of today. I don't know if that is my insanity. I know that I'm insane. The program tells us that we will be restored to sanity and my solution today is no longer drinking and using drugs. In that area I know that I am no longer insane. When I was a kid and growing up the whole thing was to get married and have children and that will make you happy. That's bullshit for me; it didn't make me happy. Nobody said happiness is an inside job.

PHILIP: If happiness is an inside job, you are referring to the fact that society creates an opposite image, the billboard approach. Madison Avenue, advertising . . . .

ANDREA: All of it. Every idea that I ever came up with; I wanted to be a lawyer, that's too grandiose. Beauty college, well you don't want to see women at their worst. Then I desperately wanted to be a writer. My high school English teacher was the only one that wanted to help me. My mother said, "That's ridiculous, what are you going to do to support yourself?" When I got married I took a writing course, a correspondence course. Of course I was using and drinking and I wrote a story about my son. It was full of self-pity. But I felt good doing it. I always had the failure thing, well screw it. I'm not good at that. Those tapes in my head would run on. Some of the stuff I wrote evidently was good. I don't know anymore. I look back on my mother and my mother even in her own eyes was a total failure. She gave to me what she had and that was nothing. Because she didn't feel she could handle her own failures, neither could I. Is my mother to blame? Hell no! That's what her mother had. People told me you got great potential and yet what's potential and where do I go to get it? Then they'd say you're a liar, a cheat, and a thief . . . and you have no backbone. I agree with them, but what do I do about it?

PHILIP: In other words, on the one hand, people around you were telling you that what you were aspiring for was just out of your league, just too much for you? At the same time, they weren't giving you support for what you actually were. They were trying to reduce you to their level sometimes?

ANDREA: Yeah, I feel like that. That occurred a couple of years ago when I went back to visit some people in my family. They weren't happy that I was growing up at all. They hated me; they couldn't stand me. The whole feeling was lie her up against the wall and shoot her down with a shotgun. She's an addict and an alcoholic. My mother today still does not approve of me. I'm not living the kind of life she wants for me to live because I let my kids go. I believe that's what my mother wanted to do too, get us out of her life so she could live. Whether that's true or not, I really don't know. But those are the feelings I have. My mother didn't want to be saddled with the responsibility, and I think if she had come out and said that and not had felt so rotten about those feelings, it would have passed for her. It passed for me. When I admitted to those horrible, icky, innermost feelings, which every human has, it's because it's human. Who wants to be saddled with a whole bunch of responsibilities, especially when you are raised to be a housewife at 17 or 18? You never lived. You never did anything but change diapers and put a bottle in a kid's mouth. That's a bummer to listen to them cry all the time and be stuck when you're only still a teenager and everybody else is out having a good time.

PHILIP: Or at least you think everyone's out playing.

ANDREA: At least you think; that's your concept of what's going on. I just happened to express it, and I put it into action. I let my children go. The kind of life I live today is an unbalanced life. People think I'm crazy because I do this type of thing. My mother doesn't approve. It doesn't matter how many clubs I could belong to or how many times my face was out in the newspaper working for other people. She wouldn't approve because I'm selfish. She told me that. You are selfish, self-centered and egotistical, all you obsessed people are. I have to agree with her. Yes, I am.

PHILIP: You mentioned before the idea of using something out there to make it better inside. What do you mean by that?

ANDREA: Well, if you look at the overall picture of people, we choose chemicals to put inside to put out the feelings, to get rid of them. Other people eat food compulsively. Their whole life surrounds food, meal times. Other people get absorbed in abstract things to forget what's going on inside so they don't have to face what's happening. Other people read, they get lost in books. They get lost in movies. That something on the outside can make it feel better on the inside. That's what I always did. All I wanted was for somebody to put a band-aide on it. The bandaides were already inside. I just couldn't find them. And then one day, goaded by pure necessity and not out of any virtue but because I was going to die, I had to stop. I had to take a look inside. People didn't want to do that because they might have to admit to their nasty little feelings they've been told they weren't supposed to feel.

So we find ourselves in the desert, and we begin to look back and see how we got here and our methods of trying to get out. This is a basic reality, that we are persons, selves that need to be loved, accepted by others *and* by our own selves. We do need to love and enjoy ourselves. And it's a lot more than a self-concept. We are far more than any "idea" about ourselves in a place and in a way beyond our thoughts and feelings, our urges, needs, wants, goals, feelings. Not being and living from our persons, our real life center, we begin to adjust to our world in an ego, I-am-an-individual, *really* separate in a way from everyone else. What are we left with? Survival. A fight, an existence, a lone struggle. We are left to our own devices. Without growing up in a loving family, we become entirely vulnerable to this most chaotic, anxiety adjustment — obsession.

Where our true self should be, our consciousness-awareness is filled with "I," resulting in an ever changing flow of obsessions. We need to possess people, things, something to make us feel better, good. These painful feelings are at their root, scars left where a self, a person should be . . . guilt, pride, lust, envy, jealousy, hate, anger, fear, insecurity . . . the absence of a person, of a love relationship. And when we're not doing what we "should," when we're not being "ourselves" . . . guilt.

Trying to fill the void through obsessive behavior only makes us more aware of our deeper pain. We find that instead of living our lives, our lives are being drawn into these compulsive-obsessive behavior patterns. We become obsessed with society normed goals, a series of events to make it all "right" . . . graduate from college, get married, have that family, rise to the top of a business, make the big money, have the big house. etc. Time, a servant of the ego, begins to take over. Indeed, we are helpless to stop the flow of events. Just try and stop drinking, overeating, gambling, lusting on our own! We say to ourselves, "I can stop whenever I want to." Well, how many of us *really* can? How many of us can rid our minds of that constant flow of ideas, that harrassment of concepts, voices bombarding us; or those emotions that strap us down and by which, so much of our behavior is determined.

The feelings and ideas arise and instead of honestly dealing with them we escape, numb them with chemicals, pills, drink, diversions, fantasies. Alcoholism, drug addiction are no more than the more self-destructive, reality distorting forms of obsession. And who among us is ready to admit to these obsessions, that we *have* lost self direction and the ability to make decisions for ourselves, that we really don't control much, that we really are something, but not the neat, dressed-up image of ourselves we had . . . that we are obsessed? And in our society obsessive behavior is so extensive that it approaches the norm.

On the bookstands a big seller is *sex;* how to do it, how to get the most out of it, where to go, and what to do to get it, what everybody else is doing in relationship to their sex lives, etc. Sum it all up and we are obsessed with sex; there is another word too, lust. We can't get our fill. Sure, a little knowledge is healthy, an accepting awareness of our own and someone else's sexual personality is good, positive, loving. But are we getting lost in the recipes and fail to do the cooking and the eating? And who really cares what the national norm is; does that add or detract one bit from the sexual love we express for those persons we care about? We're reading the wrong maps.

Underneath an obsession there is a process, a dynamic going on. It concerns the balance of our ego and our self, of what we have become in terms of our ego, of what we are doing in an everyday way to adjust to life through our egos. Out of our imbalanced ego comes the obsessions which harass us.

Two

OUR UNBALANCED, UNALIGNED EGO

Many of us have a faulty conception of just what is our ego. If you will recall a moment in your life when you felt totally whole, at peace . . . perhaps lost in an admiring gaze at some beauty of nature, you are sensing the self. In this space of "perfection" we feel a sense of well being and completeness. The self is then at our center and knows itself as completed. Soon we stir from our dream-like state and begin again the business of living. What in us becomes aware of being in the world again, of expanding energy through thought, action to get something, and which gives us the sense of "me," the individual; that is the ego. It senses itself apart from the world and begins to acknowledge reality in terms of I-they, I-it.

Our ego draws on the services of our bodies and minds. Hence when "we" feel hungry, "we" do something about it; when we feel emotions which are painful, we may seek to avoid them; when some need, real or imaginary, makes itself present to our consciousness, our minds begin the process of examining it and analyzing our environment around us for a solution to this need. These are ego functions. The ego is also aware of the conditions imposed on us by our universe; of time, in terms of past and future. And with the mind the ego creates a steady flow of ideas, an ever changing pattern of the world around us, translated into ideas, and that same world is transformed through our bodies into feelings.

Psychologists have further identified the ego states of functioning as Child-Adult-Parent. The Child ego has a positive and negative state as well as the parent ego. In the Child ego we find the positive feelings and activity of exploring one's environment, the sense of discovery, curiosity, of being cared for and nurtured, feeling secure and loved, a sense of joy, celebration, playing, running, that spirit of trust and freedom. The negative side of our Child ego has us inflexible, immobile, insecure, sad and pouting, rejected and unloved, dependent on someone, lonely.

With our Child ego the Parent ego interacts. We find these three ego states, Child-Parent-Adult, not only within us but in other people as well. Thus not only does the parent ego of someone else respond to the Child in us, but our Parent ego talks to and does business with our Child within. The positive Parent is nurturing, protective, guiding and helpful, accepting and concerned; the negative Parent is critical, creating a steady flow of do's and don't's, judgmental, comparing others, dominating and possessive, overly restrictive, and duty bound without seeing the person for whom the duty is performed.

Our Adult ego, unlike the highly emotionally charged Child-Parent states, is neutral, evaluating, looking things over to see what's really going on, a mediator between Child and Parent, reasoning, rational. It acts like a consultant to the Child-Parent in assisting them in getting what they seek.

Of course not all the time do we find the Child-Adult-Parent functioning as one team. When there is an imbalance, we really feel it, painful and confusing. The Parent can be totally dominating our Child, keeping us from enjoying ourselves, having fun, learning. It can give us such a steady diet of do, don't, I expect this, live up to this standard; this is OK, that is not OK, you're loved if, you're mine, you belong to me, etc. that our enmotional condition flares up constantly with hostility, guilt, fear, insecurity, anger, dependency. Our little Child fights back at times; then again we can cover, run and go hide.

Beneath this ego layer in our consciusness is our Self, our Person. When all is right, the ego states are functioning together in the service of the Self. They procure the well being of the whole Person, seemingly inspired by the gentle commanding presence of our Self. But with most of us this state rarely exists. Our 'Self' is either never allowed its proper reign due to our failure to receive unconditional love, or we allow it to slip beneath the waves, so to speak, and place our ego in command of our lives . . . we become Self (ego)-willed individuals for which life is a battle ground, a survival course full of fear, anxiety, mistrust and no love. We think we can do it all. One Person-to-another-Person relationships are avoided in favor of ego relationships, where we are either dependent, people pleasing, approve of and accept me, I'll follow your lead. Or we control, dominate, become above it all, independent, manipulative, power-oriented. In either case we are totally susceptible to what other people do to us and we *to* them; we react to outside forces or the whim of a chaotic inner ego. We wander the desert whose horizons are bounded by a misplaced ego.

PHILIP: Do you think you can look at what you're saying from another point of view? Society gives us identities to become or roles to play or things to do. Instead of developing an identity from ourselves from the things we do, that we feel important about, things we find really comfortable, successful and fulfilling, we adopt a whole set of other people's standards, values and directions.

ANDREA: Oh, yeah, that's definite. You didn't have any, you know when you're first born. You are raised with your parents' concepts. Your parents feed you and they give you the "You're a good girl, you're a bad girl, you don't want to do that, that isn't good enough for you." When I was born I didn't have any tapes in my head, so I believed those things. Why did I feel worthless? Because I'd been told I was worthless all my life. The first time I stood up and told my mother I wanted to be a lawyer, she laughed in my face. Then I wanted to go to beauty college . . . and she laughed in my face.

PHILIP: Why did she laugh in your face?

ANDREA: Well, a lawyer was absolutely ridiculous in their time. Do you realize how much college you need? And you're going to have to split yourself and marriage. I was raised to be a wife, I wasn't raised to be a career woman. Not until I was a senior in high school did my mother ever bring up the fact that I might just have to go to work. I'd always been raised to be a good wife, nothing else.

PHILIP: Are you saying there is a real conflict in people's lives, that parent what parents and the immediate people around you were saying and what you actually wanted for yourself were two different things? And possibly this confusion might lend itself to people taking alcohol as a relief from the conflict created between others telling you what you can do and can't do . . . and what *you* want to do?

ANDREA: Yes, but I think it was the way I accepted it. I was a very wishy-washy weak kid. I have a sister who is perfectly normal. She did not go with the career she wanted. She wanted to be a gynecologist. Instead, she chose marriage. She would have been a fantastic gynecologist. She had the mind to do it. She is around forty now but in those days women didn't do those things; men did. I don't have the faintest idea what the confrontation between my mother and her was. I just know that when I came up with "I want to be a lawyer," that was an impossibility. Why don't you be a secretary like I am? I didn't want to be a secretary. I hated the fact of sitting in front of a typewriter and doing the same thing over and over. My mother on the one hand implied I was stupid while the school was saying I had a higher I.Q. than most . . . and my potential was fantastic. That's all well and good, but where do I direct it? There wasn't anybody willing to direct me anyway to anything that I felt I wanted.

It seems to me, through the way I have known myself, that when I experience the simple reality of "I am," then my self is in the center of my being. Yet when I complete the statement, "I am . . . a teacher, a resident of California," etc., my consciousness moves away from real self, into limiting confines of an idea, the idea, or identity I have *about* myself. Through the process of becoming an identity, an idea, we begin relating and adjusting to life, not from our true command center of "Self," but the description we have of us, the standards we set, the goals and plans we have made for ourselves. And the longer we do this bit of tape recording our identity, acting on ideas, we increasingly see reality as consisting mainly of ideas and emotions originating from the interaction of our Child-Parent egos.

Another form of this idea making, identifying process, is role playing. I am a teacher, therefore I will act like a teacher should and is expected to act. I am a single person, thus I will act like a "single" individual; or I am a wife or husband, I'll act like one. Our lives move away from being lived and created from our inner self.

Other variations and consequences of being an idea and experiencing ideas as real include:

race identitiy	"I'm a Chicano," a "Black," I'll act like one.

religious identity	"I'm a Protestant, my religion is better than you Catholics, and visa versa . . . religion camparing.
sex identity	I'm a liberated woman, I'll go out and get a career . . . it's expected.
comparisons	Am I good enough to meet these "standards" of what I should be?
self-worth game	Am I acceptable to you, to myself; I've been everything you expected, did all that I should have done.
	I know this person, I've been there, I own this, I can do that . . . therefore, I'm OK, better than you.

To illustrate just how real ideas can be, I've asked students to sit with their eyes shut. While doing that I'll talk to them, "What did you experience in the present moment?" Some say they heard my voice, most are thinking they experienced nothing, even though I talked the entire time. Then I ask the same question and touch them, and most respond to the direct experience of being touched. Finally I ask, "Based only on what you are presently experiencing; in this here and now moment, through a direct experience, answer for me, which sex are you?" Most everyone says the expected answer of male-female. But I protest this answer and draw their attention to what they directly experienced that indicated to them the validity of their answer. Sitting in a chair is certainly not a function of maleness or femaleness. Take this example to its practical applications and we find that we do take ideas, identities, standards, expectations, judgments as all real. They are ideas, concepts, but we give them flesh, and often power over us.

Once involved in this network of ideas and feelings we seek solutions to our general state of emptiness and anxiety and answers to our longings. Thus begins the chasing of your tail, the game of "recipe collecting." We want to find out "why," "what's going on?" But we are trapped. Answers are only *ideas,* another set of ideas to add to our collection. We begin frantically reading books, attending seminars, lectures, talking late into the night of our discontent. Meanwhile, like the starving man collecting recipes, we remain hungry. Much of psychology today is aimed at the ego, providing ego oriented solutions in the form of idea-awareness, and strokes.

A critical result of idea-answer searching is that we avoid any responsibility for what we have done to ourselves. Instead, the answers to our "why's?" places the burden on the ideas we discover . . . all this a subtle form of the classic ego defense . . . rationalizing. Or we just may enter upon a dependent follower relationship with someone giving us all those "answers," allowing us to continue to avoid ourselves. Rarely do we find the "right" recipe, actually go through all the work of balancing our egos, putting the self in the center of things . . . cooking us something we can sink our teeth into, satisfy our famished hunger. Rarer still do we *eat,* partake of the real thing.

A kind of insanity settles over us at this point. We really cannot see what we are doing, that it is hurting us and others. Obsessions run rampant in this situation. They are the ego's way of giving us our "solutions." Were there a proper relationship of ego being in harmony with a centered self, obsessions could never come into being. Our insanity does not allow us to see this. Instead we take control, seek to control everyone and everything in our lives. We believe we can do things we cannot do, be things we are not, see things that do not exist, fail to recognize things as they are, and live with the mistaken notion that people do things to us.

When we know our self in our "middle," we know once and for all, we *are* OK. But with our self displaced by our ego, we seek obsessively to receive those strokes of I'm OK, tell me I'm OK, do this for me to make me feel OK. We really *do* care then about what other people think about us, act towards us. We hand over our blank chalkboards and give them permission write on it whatever they want . . . we, of course, react to every word as if Gospel.

There is another angle in recognizing an ego controlling us. Many people say "I don't want to do this alone, go here alone, take this class alone, attend this party alone, etc." And I'm not talking about those of us who would rather *share* with someone else. No, I'm referring to those of us who would really like to do such-and-such but because we don't have anyone there to hold our hand we just won't do things. This is known as plugging into people, wanting them to do our living for us, making our decisons, do our growing for us. The misplaced Child ego is in search of a Parent. We fail to realize that it is our feet that must do the walking to reach the Promised Land.

Because of what we feel and think, we find ourselves feeling guilty over what we actually *do.* We live with constant guilt and if initially we don't feel guilty, we end up doing so. Our egos just love to "judge." Suppose you were cooking a real fancy meal for someone and the highlight of this dinner was a cherry cheese cake you had baked. And someone unknown to you helps himself to a slice. It comes time for your dessert and upon opening the refrigerator you behold the cheese cake absent a slice. Now you can do one of two things: Either blow up and go storming around looking for the culprit who just "ruined" your perfect creation, or simply observe that a slice is missing. This says nothing about the consequences of that piece being absent, of your underlying fear of how you may appear to others. This need not happen because we do not judge reality if our selves are centered, we merely observe it for what it is. The Self, it turns out, does not judge reality; rather it recognizes, accepts, acts on it.

In the absence of our true Self, our ego obsessively escapes through fantasy and imagination. We imagine ourselves to possess qualities we do not have. We create unrealistic goals for ourselves, thereby moving us out of the present moment where the self resides into the future, where our ego presides. On entanglements of preconceptions, expectations are woven, setting us up for guilt, disappointment, and frustrations when things don't go our way, do not become realized. Goals and the like really don't exist save as an idea. I cannot live in the goal, I must live in this present moment. It becomes a succession of present moments through which any "goal" becomes completed anyway.

The flow of ideas and feelings from our egos through our consciousness for many people is a perpetual harassment. Yet we fail to see that we are attached to this flow, we will it, want it, choose it and even focus our attention to our favorite concepts and emotions to which we become attached and by which we become obsessed. We are obsessed by our emotions, addicted to them, desire them, feel out of sorts if we don't have them. This is why so many of us either keep coming back to people, relationships, situations which are filled with painful, negative or very pleasurable feelings, or remain in situations where all we continue to experience are feelings which get us nowhere and cause us a great deal of anguish. Obsessions control us, we do not control obsessions.

We will consider one last illusion our ego presents us with, the idea that we possess anything. She's my wife, this is my car, that's my job, etc. Do we really possess anything or is it merely an idea in our minds which we exchange with other people for the convenience of functioning in our everyday world? If we possess something, where do we have it? Our lovers, husbands, wives, are they not free to walk out of our lives at anytime? Our looks can change, our jobs, the elements claim any material object we "own." Yet the ego perpetrates this notion of "possession," giving us one more mode of living from the point of view of our ego.

Other books have been written much more in depth concerning our ego and its function, differences, mannerisms. Our purpose here is to recognize that obsessions and obsessive, addictive behavior spring up when the ego is not in harmony with our self, when the ego has replaced our self and we do not know experience and function from our real self. No solutions of and from the ego, nor any degree or amount of ego satisfaction can realign our self with our ego. The solution to life in harmony lies elsewhere.

Three

THE OBSESSIONS OF ALCOHOLISM, DRUG ADDICTION

PHILIP: Do you feel in your past you've had too many people waiting in the wings to ambush you?

ANDREA: Yes, I guess so. I don't even know if that is valid. I just think that is part of my sickness. But it had to come from some place. I wasn't born with it.

PHILIP: As long as you or anyone else felt that way there would be a tremendous amount of stifling of yourself, a tremendous amount of holding back, a tremendous amount of apprehension, of fear and anxiety.

ANDREA: Yeah, I'm beginning to realize that's what I've lived under the last two years. Unconsciously, up until last night, I had waited for the other shield to drop and now I fully expected it to drop. There is always a sense of relief after I've gotten mad, and then it's like now you've really told me how you feel about me. So now I know where I'm at and I can function in there. I cannot function when people like me.

PHILIP: It sounds as if you took the cautious way and instead of asserting yourself and communicating your feelings or your apprehensions, you waited for somebody to do it for you.

ANDREA: Yeah, and then I'd tuck my tail and run.

PHILIP: Do you find a lot of alcoholics or people using alcohol and drugs as an escape for their feelings,as one of their defense mechanisms of avoiding feelings, of merely being passive about the whole thing?

ANDREA: I really don't know that. I know that I've been told since I've been in AA that I'm not different, so there's got to be alcoholics that feel the same way I do. But I wouldn't say people I've run into really are that passive. I don't know. I can't answer that. I've been praying. I've stayed in prayer for three days, constant prayer. "Please God, be there when I go down that pit." I keep trying to look at the positive side because I really feel that it is totally arrogant. I don't think I've felt this worthless since I was drinking. I feel just absolutely raw, and scared to death; absolutely terrified.

PHILIP: And you find it difficult to pinpoint exactly the cause of this fear?

ANDREA: The only thing I can think of goes back to my not being worth anything. I have no self-worth at all. Everytime I start to feel better about me, I set something up to punish myself one more time.

ANNE: You find a lot of obsessive masturbators, too. An awful lot of addicts and narcotics have a tremendous amount of guilt because they continuously masturbate. They have a tremendous amount of guilt about it, and they don't understand why they do it. It's a part of comfort and most people, because of their upbringing and their background, sleeping around is a no-no and that and whatever has been laid on them. Anybody that has ever masturbated knows that following masturbation or following an orgasm there is a period or feeling of well-being, of wholeness. And so rather than go out and be naughty and sleep around and just screw anybody, they do it to themselves. That is also a part of the alcoholic and addict: Obsessive-compulsive personalities, tremendous amount of control. They don't have to open themselves up to anybody. They can comfort themselves. I have heard obsessive-compulsive people state that, when they got to the point in their own self-examination and open enough to express what's real, what's really going on inside of them. If they really don't need anybody, which is the whole idea, "I don't want to need anybody," "I don't want to put myself in a position for rejection," they can even have sex with themselves. "Nobody else is going to love me, I'll love me." The feelings of this sense of relief and this sense of well-being is very similar to taking a drink or dropping a pill or what I imagine people feel when they gamble or whatever they do, whatever the reason.

PHILIP: What does insane mean to you?

ANDREA: Thinking that I'm going to have a problem, or I'm emotionally upset . . . and I'm trying to cope with something that I can't cope with. My answer is that no longer will a drink make it better. It will be different this time. It's like the first time a person ever got drunk and threw up violently but couldn't wait to do it again! That's insanity, and it's crazy to think like that. People that don't have the disease, and I believe the mental obsession comes first, because you've got to have it mentally before you pour it into your system . . . to drink and throw up and make a fool of themselves. The nonalcoholic won't do that again. He won't drink and drive if he's been in an accident before. But an alcoholic will get behind the wheel every time. It will be different *this* time, he tells himself.

PHILIP: You said that the mental obsession comes first. Is this something of a definition for alcoholism?

ANDREA: Yes, the definition that I was given is that alcoholism is a mental obsession, coupled with a physical allergy of the body. I take the drink mentally first, obviously, because I have to tell my hand to pick up the glass and drink it with the thought that it's going to be different this time. I can handle it and nothing will happen; it's just one drink to relax.

PHILIP: Then you don't buy the idea that a person is physically impelled once the drinking process has started, that the body controls the mind? Or do you believe that the mind still has a starting basis for a person's drinking? In other words, what is the proper relationship, as you see it, between the power of the allergy of the body versus the mental obsession? Is one superior to the other, or do they go perfectly fifty percent hand in hand?

ANDREA: The way I see it is that the mind controls the whole thing. Your mind has power over your body, your mind tells you what your body is going to do. Without your mind, you're not going to move. My mind had to tell me it was okay. I justified it and rationalized it. My insanity told me that it was going to be different, and one drink was going to make it better. Maybe I could face it better. As an alcoholic, once I put the alcohol in my system, I believed that we have an "I care" center in our brain and that alcohol goes there and then "I don't care." When I drank one, it's not going to hurt to drink another. That's nuts with my background, with an alcoholic's background. An alcoholic will be fine and won't be thinking about anything in particular. Then maybe he'll pass a billboard and think, "Yeah, a beer looks good."

That sets off the thing in their head, in my head. Then I go through the whole trip. Automatically now, because I've been sober for so long, but I've been sober long enough to realize that I have to play the trip all the way through. Sure, the first beer is going to taste good. But what's going to happen with the second, the third, the fourth, the fifth, the sixth?

PHILIP: You talked about society having this defect, this conditioning effect on us. Do you think that one of the contributing factors of people turning to drink is the fact that they have too many alternatives? Too many things to pick from. Too much stimuli coming into their minds?

ANDREA: I don't know. I don't like to blame society for my disease. As a kid you see your parents uptight and you see them relax. They come home from work and the first thing is I think I'll have a drink to relax. I was raised in an alcoholic family; my mom and dad. My mother was totally insane and she didn't drink. In the one time I saw her drunk, she was even worse. I always said that I wasn't going to drink. The first I had was purely for medicinal purposes, but it was magic. It was the magic that took the pain inside away, wiped it out. I was able to sleep for the first time in nine years. Comfortably enough, not scared. Now I don't know at that point, when I was nine years old, whether I identified booze with pain, police, blood, throwing up, fighting and screaming, or insanity. The thing I hear today is you are not sophisticated enough if you don't drink. I sat one night listening to commercials and when they were over I was a dead beat because I didn't use Lady Clairol on my hair, didn't use a certain kind of lipstick, was supposed to look sophisticated with a cocktail in my hand. I laughed because I didn't exist as a "woman." I don't exist because I don't do the things they are telling me to do that will make me beautiful and wonderful. Luckily, I am now able to laugh at that. But as kids are growing up, they have peer group pressure on them. You're not "cool" unless you smoke a joint. You're not "cool" if you can't guzzle a beer down.

. . . . She'd say things about my Dad and then all of a sudden she would do a switch around and then it wasn't his fault. None of it ever made any sense to me, ever. It was like one thing was said and some place along the line she'd either started to grow and change and never let us in on it. I wasn't given the script. Somebody didn't hand out the script to me. Like I missed something; I keep missing. I feel that way all the time. That has not changed for me at all. Even in AA it has not changed. The thing that I've tried to do is cope with it and go along with it but there's times when I just feel like to hell with it. That's where I'm at right now, obviously. I don't understand, I just don't understand.

PHILIP: What you are saying is that there is a way in which things happen in society you weren't told about?

ANDREA: Yeah, I feel like they forgot to tell me. I've always felt like the child that was kind of ignored and swished away. Ignore her, she's okay,

PHILIP: Like there were expectations laid on you but they didn't tell you what they really expected and then when you didn't come up to it they jumped all over you?

ANDREA: Yeah, exactly. When I was nine years old, and that's when I first began drinking, I was expected to act like a 21 year old; had the responsibility of taking care of the home, doing all those things and yet I was treated in a different manner. But if I didn't live up to those things, you know the basic things of: "Andrea, clean the house," and I'm standing there like that's groovy but how do I clean the house? So I would take it upon myself to clean it the way I thought it should be cleaned, but it never matched up to what my mother wanted. But my mother never bothered to show me. I always wondered what are you yelling at me for?

PHILIP: What you're describing is a condition that lends itself to a lot of feelings of inadequacy as well as total confusion.

ANDREA: I always felt inadequate because I never matched up, I never made it. Why can't you be like your sister?

PHILIP: In other words, what you're saying Andrea, is that people have it in their heads expectations that are not communicated to the people that are affected by those expectations?

ANDREA: I believe that. I don't like crying out "poor me, mommy didn't treat me right." She did the best she could 'cause that's the way she was raised. She couldn't possibly have done any better. It isn't just parents. It's the whole thing; it's school, society, you know the right hand never knows what the left hand is doing because they never get together and talk about it.

PHILIP: So really, in a final analysis, when a person feels the problem of alcoholism or drug abuse, the decision is theirs whether or not they really want to change. If they don't make that decison, nothing will happen.

ANDREA: Most definitely. I believe in my beliefs, the things I know, God is a loving God and He isn't going to push His way into your life unless you want Him. He's not going to fight, beat down the door to get you. I'm not going to either. If you want it, why waste my time. I don't like arguments, it's tiring and I don't have enough energy to do it. When you make the decision, then you have a chance. But up until that point there isn't one. Needing some help is different than wanting it. Knowing you need it is only admittance, not acceptance. If you don't accept it, you can admit 'til doomsday and nothing will happen.

PHILIP: How do people who are *not* alcoholics face their problems, cover up whatever is going on?

ANDREA: I don't think they do. I think that the thing that shows that they don't is ulcers, heart attacks, nerves, acid indigestion, migraine headaches, everything. All the diseases are caused mentally. That shows me that there aren't a hell of a lot out there facing their problems. They take a lot of Rolaids and a lot of Malox and go to a lot of doctors and take a lot of tranquilizers. That's how they face their problems. They can go around and handle it I guess without going down into the depths of alcoholism and drug addiction. In the long run they escape some place—into fantasy, into movies, into TV, into work; people that work constantly because they can't face their home life. I don't think anyone, without some kind of program, faces his problems. He fights them. But somewhere along the line, when he gets old and thinks about dying, he turns to God. And he talks about God all the time.

PHILIP: Do you think that one of the identities,the little child in us, has really been squashed? Do you find among alcoholics, users, and even recovered alcoholics that they need a little child to play so as to be spontaneous?

ANDREA: I think the little child is beaten to death, it's squashed. The alcoholics and abusers I've known have their little child so covered up and so denied and so hated that it's been for me a very painful process to let my kid out and let her play and tell her when she's throwing a temper tantrum that you don't do that anymore. We are immediately from birth told to mature. Why aren't you walking yet? God, I wish you'd get potty trained! You're more of a pain in the ass than anything. Get out of my way. I watched a little girl the other day five years old, in a brand new area of the desert, coming from the big city into all this space out here. The girl is let off the bus. She's been shown the way once; she tells her mommy she knows how to get home. Nothing looks familiar and she's totally confused. Mommy calls me to go pick her up. I'm glad to pick up the little girl. I have sympathy, I identify with those little kids. There she is with tears running down her face and it's hotter than hell. She's not used to the desert heat, she's totally terrified but she can't tell mommy because mommy's going to get mad at her. I picked her up and drove her home and her mom said, "I'm really pissed at you," and pushed her out of the way; never hugged her, never said anything. It embarassed her to have to call me to come and get the kid. It had nothing to do with the kid, it had to do with the broad's inadequacy . . . embarassed that she hadn't taught her daughter well enough. The only reason I could identify with the mother is because I was a mother who did that. The little girl just wanted to be loved; just a hug and a pat on the head. But her mother was incapable of doing it, totally incapable because she doesn't like the kid. The kid is a hassel, the kid is a responsibility. But she couldn't wait to get pregnant and have a baby. After that . . . as woman being pregnant, that's the only way I felt whole.

Probably the most obvious and destructive obsession occuring in our society is alcoholism, drug addiction and abuse. If conservative estimates are correct, then 15 million Americans are alcoholics and possibly as many use drugs of some sort to ease the pain of everyday living. This statistic is brutal enough, but coupled with it is the estimate that 60 million people are directly affected by who the alcoholic-drug user is and does.

The process and dynamics of this obsession are similar to any other obsession; however, the degree and intensity of these obsessions are overpowering, coming in the form of complete lack of control and a mind whose insanity clouds its victim with the most impenetrable and erroneous self-deceptions.

After working with teenage alcoholics for several years I saw a basic pattern emerge. The obsession of alcohol and drugs, like every other obsession, begins with a shift of consciousness-awareness away from self-identity to an ego identity. Conditional love or no love at all given or witheld from the child, or a steady exchange of open hostilities, rejection, and abuse creates the feeling and image in the child of "I'm no good, I'm not OK, I'm bad and deserve only to be hurt and to suffer, I'm helpless." Through childhood, into adolescence and adulthood, these feelings intensify, expand into fear, anger, and depression. The fear comes from not being and knowing a secure self, being time-ego oriented to concerns of the past and future, of no confidence that "I can handle it, make responsible decisions for my own well being," and failing to establish open personal relationships with the important people in our life. Anger is the expression of this total frustration of the self being abandoned, repressed and dethroned in favor of the performance oriented ego, whose Child-Parent emotional states run amuck! The anger builds into an open hostility and defensiveness towards "them," people around us. The real suffering, however, is when we turn that anger in, towards ourselves. We do this because deep down we *are* completely frustrated, our real self hidden in the basements of consciousness, and it wants out! Depression, in a sense, is a real cry for help from the self, which is saying "Why are you doing this to me, don't you know who I am, *that* I am!" Everytime we are depressed, thus angry at ourselves, we are not being true to our real self, and it *is* going to let us know about it.

The process places our fragile egos in a most vulnerable place. From our position here we can pick from the following strategies of feeling, thinking:

> I'm not OK . . . hurt me, I'll hurt myself, I don't deserve to feel good.
>
> What do you think of me? Am I doing what you want, am I pleasing you? Am I acceptable?
>
> I don't want to play, with you, or anyone.

Those people, those other people are so sick..

If only I could have . . . .

If only this would have happened.

This developing alcoholic-obsessive personality finds himself constantly deluged with feelings he doesn't want. Well, what do we do if we are experiencing an uncomfortable, painful feeling? How do we escape, repress, deny, cover it up? Do we anesthetize it with alcohol and drugs, tranquilizers to make it feel OK? If our obsession is strong enough, we hurt deeply enough, and our sense of reality is distorted enough, then we drink. At this point we are "insane." We begin our new found track career as a long distance runner. We run from every and any feeling we don't want to deal with, and the course is endless, unto death do us part for many.

This life and death struggle to those whose obsessive natures have not taken the alcohol and drug route, may seem an over dramatization . . . it's not. As the disease of alcoholism progresses, the consuming feeling of unworthiness expands and deepens. The ego presents the image to the alcoholic that in every way he's *not* OK. So what do you do to someone who is completely rotten? You kill them . . . one drinks oneself to death.

The alcoholic, drinking too much, too often, does not have the outward symptoms of drinking as the root of his problem. This rather is the result, the effect of other dynamics. We are still talking about an obsession and the obsessed personality taken to its extreme. As such we can identify the following obsessive-compulsive personality traits with the alcoholic; a list which extends to obsessive behavior in general:

Running. Tranquilizing his feelings, suppressing unwanted emotions, denying his experiences.

Insanity. Fails to see what he is doing, admits to his real motives or the consequences of his obsession. Denies any responsibility for his feelings, actions; people, places and things are the cause, he contends, of his problems. Seeks a solution through people, places, things. Usually reality is a combination of unwanted feelings and ideas which are prejudicial. Relationships of an open, sharing nature are nonexistent as is any kind of "personal" reality, i.e., love, acceptance, sharing, concern, playful interaction. Expectations, do's and don'ts, judgments, erroneous ideas occupy the mind.

Helplessness, lack of control. The person is actually powerless over his drinking obsession but believes in a self-deceptive way that he has total control and thus seeks to extend that control over people around him . . . manipulation of people, situations.

Total Self-Ego Centeredness. No one else counts. His life and problems are the extent of his awareness, participation in life. His satisfaction is the major concern, and he remains out of touch.

Not a "nice" person, the "help me" game. Professional people helping the obsessed alcoholic often play into his hands as he presents himself as the abused, suffering victim of some catastrophic event. So they comfort him and some would even attempt to rescue him. All the while the "victim" is thinking what a dummy this guy is and how to manipulate him. So many with this obsession view themselves as above it all and superior in every way to whomever they come in contact with.

Fantasy. Instead of dealing with what actually is, what could be and might have been takes on an escapist appeal. It remains difficult to apply oneself to the everyday tasks that remain in front of this personality. Delusions of false strengths, exaggerated weaknesses and of who one really is abound.

Making it better inside with things outside. Things never feel good, or good enough on the inside. A general feeling of uneasiness, incompleteness, anxiety, unsatisfied needs or wants prevails. Consequently, there is an attempt to make it feel good within by drink, or any other thing, person, place that seems to satisfy for a time. The search is endless, the solutions diverse and only momentarily satisfying.

Nonparticipation. An obsessed individual, especially the alcoholic, does not take part in life, does not participate.He becomes the casual observer, side-lining it in favor of those more "put together, capable souls" who are "better" that he. His ego-centeredness makes him susceptible to comparisons, judgments, ridicule, and his own self-imposed inferiority so why get involved with all that coming down on you? His playful child remains buried.

Childishness. Especially with the obsession of alcohol, the progression of the disease process takes the individual further and further away from emotional maturity and isolates his consciousness into his negative child ego The adult ego state fails to develop, hence childish emotional behavior and assertions freely exhibit themselves. The attitude prevails of "I want what I want when I want it." Reason and responsibility becomes replaced by by compulsive whim. From another point of view the positive, playful child also is denied his expression. A most obvious, glaring trait, deficiency with the obsessed alcoholic is the inability to play, to enjoy, to have fun. So who wants to sober up, drop our obsessions if once we get sober we can't enjoy living? The obsessed alcoholic remains an individual in search of his unborn, unlived happy child.

Self-punishment, guilt. The deep-seated despising of self, the result of failing to receive unconditional love, and the repression of our true self in favor of our ego, brings the individual to living a life-style of self-punishment. If something "good" happens, he'll chastize himself, drink to excess, and then wallow in the guilt of having failed, or as often is the case, experiencing the guilt for just being alive, just being born.

Resentment. The adult ego being absent in the obsessed alcoholic, and unwanted feelings a constant concern of his, this individual represses feelings that should be healthfully expressed when, where, and to whom they concern. Buried, they become resentments, festering sores of unexpressed hostility, leading to states of aggravated depression.

Self-justification. With the obsessed person, and especially the alcoholic, actions and decisions, responsible behavior all done for the growing well-being and adjustments to life of the person are severely limited. In fact, these have no "person" or "self" from which to proceed, it being buried and the ego taking its place. With this state of affairs all a person can do is make excuses for his ego-oriented behavior, defending the last cause of his growing self-destruction. An endless flow of justified behavior and rationalizations follow.

Four

RELATIONSHIPS, MEN-WOMEN, SEX: IN SEARCH OF A FEELING

PHILIP: Looking back over your being alcoholic, both using and in the process of recovery, how has this affected your relationships with men?

ANDREA: Total disaster. As a practicing woman alcoholic, obsessive-compulsive, and even after I quit drinking, the relationships were the same. I was still dealing with the same mental problems I had before. Up to this date, the relationships have all been the same. I've grown a little bit and seen myself and my own character defects: the demanding, the insecurity, the lack of self-worth, just the whole composite of what I am as an alcoholic, never being able to admit that I never was in love, that I really was in heat; never being able to admit that I really didn't know a damn thing of what love was all about. I figured that if I did the right thing, then he would love me. Then I came to the point in my life where that isn't right, that isn't enough. Now I'm scared to find out if I really am what I am. Some days I really don't feel like putting a nice meal on the table. I have always overcompensated for what I thought were my inadequacies, always."

PHILIP: "You mention this idea about pleasing your mate, that they will love you if you do this and that. That is called people pleasing. How do you react to that?"

ANDREA: I identify with that. I have always people-pleased the people that I've disliked the most. I'm the type of human being that will walk into a room with a hundred people, ninety-nine of them will love me and one will hate me. I will go to that one person and demand that he like me . . . and I will do what he wants me to do to get him to like me. There is never enough love. There is never enough of anything. I don't do that like I used to because I'm aware of it. I've become more outspoken and today I get a kick out of people who dislike me. I don't know if that is a character defect.

I can be pretty blatant with my statements. I have a hard time sugar-coating the truth today. It's getting a little bit easier so that I won't hurt somebody and alienate them. I people-pleased everybody I knew because I never felt that I was doing the right thing. Therefore, I had to overcompensate in another area. I was never perfect in any area I had to be.

PHILIP: Do you think that is a generalized trait of an alcoholic?

ANDREA: Yes, I believe so. I believe that the majority of us are, or they go the opposite way with the screw you attitude when inside they are hurt, lonely, and scared. They say it doesn't matter when in fact it matters a hell of a lot. The thing that started setting me free from people-pleasing was when I quit denying the fact that it mattered. It did matter; but now it doesn't matter that it matters. I don't feel that I have a whole lot of friends today. But I do know there are people in my world that really do care and respect me. They are glad that I stand up and speak my own truth.

PHILIP: Do you feel that you should have a lot of friends?

ANDREA: No, not really. My mom told me when I was a little kid, and I guess I hung on to it, that I would be very privileged if I was to have one friend in my whole life that was really close to me. That's the only thing I ever wanted: Just one friend that I could be completely myself with no matter what it was; tell everything and know every nook and cranny of my heart. That's all I ever wanted and today I have one. I don't know if that is a stable attitude, or saying that there never could be any more.

PHILIP: Maybe that's being realistic in terms of the way people really are.

ANDREA: It could be though I never really thought about it. Every time I had a friend I felt I was betrayed in the end. It took me all this time to finally open up to one other human being completely. I find it's a little easier now to do it. There are several other people that know me pretty well but not as well as that other person.

PHILIP: When you look at a man, someone you enter a relationship with, who do you see or what role do they play? What were they doing in your life?

ANDREA: They weren't doing anything in my life. What did I see? I saw somebody to protect me, to make me better. They ruled my world. If they were miserable, then I was miserable. If they were happy, I was happy. My whole identity was wrapped up in them. I knew I existed if there was someone there. If they told me I was pretty, then I was pretty. If they told me tht I made their skin crawl, then I made their skin crawl. I was just them. I didn't have anything of my own inside. My first husband, and all the men following, were just like my father. They couldn't give anything emotionally. My dad was never around. I remember seeing my dad in instances, but he was never really around. Somehow, through the years, through all the relationships, all the men have been just like him. It made it easy for me to love the men when I wanted to because they weren't loving me ever. They didn't give me anything emotionally, but financially they did.

PHILIP: So men in their relationships were an extension of this idea of people or things outside will make it better inside?

ANDREA: Yeah, it has always been that way. Anything to fix the inside. I was told that a man would make me happy, and when he didn't make me happy I didn't understand why. I constantly depended on them for everything. Then one day I woke up and realized that wasn't true, that if I wasn't alright by myself, I wasn't going to be alright with anybody else. That was a scary place for me. Somebody said in a meeting one night that we were born alone. We came into this world alone and we are going to leave alone. I went home and threw up. That's how dependent I was on people and places and things to make me happy. I guess I was a couple of years sober by then. But I faced it, and looked at it, and I started working at it. I didn't want to use another man. We hear women say that men use women all the time when in reality the women use the men. They don't want to see that. There isn't any way that I can see a man using me unless I am using him. I use men for the sexual things, financial security, emotional security, everything. Now I come to find out that there is no such thing as emotional security—it's emotional balance. I threw up over that, too.

PHILIP: Do you think there are a lot of so-called normal women, somewhat obsessed, who really are not to the stage of practicing alcoholism, but feel the same way?

ANDREA: Yes, I do. I believe there are all kinds of housewives out there that maybe are not drinking a lot, but need a tranquilizer to put them to sleep at night. My most favorite commercial in the whole world is: This poor lady is standing over her washing machine which is bubbling over with soap suds, her dishwasher is falling apart, she's pregnant, she's got two little kids running around in diapers ruining her wet floor, and she's in tears. This voice then comes across the TV and says, "Your husband loved you so much that he gave you all this, and we love you so much that we're giving you this." He hands her a bottle of aspirin. That was my life and I believe that is a whole bunch of housewives' lives. We think the career woman will do better, so we dump the family. That isn't it. There's got to be something inside. There's got to be something for us to feel worthwhile. I felt at times that there had to be something more than bottles and diapers. There just had to be. I never could find it. There was never a program and I don't mean just A.A. There was nothing to fill that hole inside. I didn't know there was a spiritual thing because we are spiritual beings. I didn't know that, I didn't want to hear it. God had rejected me by putting me on this earth. That was the ultimate rejection when He put me here. I felt that I was doing a prison term and that everything that I did in my life was punishment. I see that desperate, horrible loneliness in so many housewives. When the husbands go off to work, it's groovy for a while and they finally find some time to be alone and relax. They turn the TV on and get involved in soap operas to fill that lonely gap inside. If they're not getting along with their husbands, their husbands come home and they're dreading it and then the fight is on. Why don't they get a divorce? They say they love their husbands. That's bullshit! They hate themselves. How can they love anybody else? If you hate yourself, you don't have a chance. We treat ourselves shabbily. Housewives will deny themselves little things like bubble baths, the right kind of color toilet paper for their bathrooms. Those are the niceties that as a housewife I did without because I didn't deserve them. My husband got his clothes washed and ironed first. They were always taken care of first. I came last because I had to overcompensate for my own inadequacies I felt as a woman. I wasn't prepared to be a woman. Nobody gave me a preparedness for that kind of life. They just told me that I was supposed to do that and it would make me happy. It's one of the biggest lies in the world. It isn't that I don't believe in marriage and families and all that. But if you go into marriage a half person, you're going to stay a half person. If you're not a whole human being, you haven't got a chance.

PHILIP: What do you see as being a whole human being?

ANDREA: Somebody that doesn't need another human being. If somebody adds something to me as a human being, I'm screwed. If they enhance my life and my world, that's nice. But if they add to me and if they leave they take part of me, I'm dead. That means that I'm not a whole human being. If I'm not okay by myself, and functioning within my own self, I'm not going to be okay if there is a man in my life. Or I can be in a whole room of people and it's still not going to be okay. I'm still looking for something out there to make it better. The bandages are inside; all the answers are within ourselves. Books really don't have the answers. They awaken what we already know within ourselves. They are a kind of tool to awaken all this knowledge that we are born with. I sometimes feel that I'm getting back to what I had when I was born. All the truth that was in me then that was smashed out of me from society through the years. We hear that old stupid statement, "out of the mouths of babes." That's true! A kid will pop up with the truth and parents likely will be embarassed. They were told that was a no-no. You listen to a kid and he's got the answer. Listen to a five year old kid. They have the answer but we smack them and say that isn't right. That's embarassing; you just embarassed your mommy. The whole feeling about that is big deal! Listen to them; you might get the message of living from a five year old kid. Watch a two year old sitting in a little sandbox. He's got the answers. He'll tell you when he's umcomfortable. He'll tell you when he's got wet pants and he won't be embarassed. He'll cry and he'll tell you that he's hungry. You ask a little kid to do something. A little girl was out here one day and I said why don't you get a glass of milk from so and so. She walked into the kitchen. Pretty soon she came back and said she was too scared to ask for a glass of milk. What adult would come out and say I'm afraid or intimidated to ask for something? Could you go with me and hold my hand? There is nobody that would do something like that except a kid. Adults will say that's stupid to feel like that. I shouldn't feel that way. That's where I see it begin. It is starting to squash that little kid. You shouldn't be scared.

During the course of our lives we engage in an ever changing involvement with people, an entering and exiting through relationships. Any one of us could say that from experiencing the following kinds of relationships:

We learned something of who, and what we were, what our society amd culture is, its roles for us to play, the options it presents us to choose from in becoming and being who we are.

We experience love and the reality of person, "other self." We learned the personal expressions of ourselves through relationships as love, security, acceptance, patience, identity, responsibility, joy, appreciation, thanksgiving. We shared and played together, found out we were worthwhile and loveable in ourselves.

We had certain needs fulfilled and explored the extent and quality of these needs . . . sex, importance, identity, being desired, dependencies, independencies, the relief of boredom, creating and living out a life style, the security of having or belonging to a someone and a stable situation.

We learned lessons, always lessons of life of what our deeper, truer self is and not just our ego states and functionings. We come to know the truth of our own aloneness, of self-love, of the gentle, fulfilling possibilities we have to live, love, laugh . . . freedom.

Throughout this process, however, few of these happenings appear orderly. Chaos and hostitlity, communication problems and frustrations, misunderstandings, fears, power struggles and intense suffering, depression and despair, hopes and longings; these mark the landscapes of our relationships. In truth, these cannot be avoided, they being the human condition, the acts and scenarios we must play before the drama finishes to a worthwhile resolve. And in a real sense we, each of us, are like a young apple tree newly planted. It may take seven years before we bear fruit, as so much has to happen before even the first fruit comes in its due season. An accepting patience is necessary as we struggle through the painful lessons of relationships:

No one has us, owns us, possesses us, nor do we anyone else. That we feel this way is an illusion of our ego replacing our true self.

Feelings are to be accepted, worked with, enjoyed, but not attached to, addicted to and obsessed by.

The form and manner of our relating to someone changes; that one Self, Person meets another, does not.

We really *are* free, complete and whole unto ourselves. It takes a lifetime of relationships to learn this.

But with proper consideration there are some soils with a chemical unbalance making it difficult or impossible to bear fruit. Insects, diseases, natural calamity befall the growing tree and order must be restored to insure the proper developments of we, "the tree." No one would deny that certain care, nutrients, and favorable growing conditions bring about an earlier first fruit, and fruit that is superior in quality, size, and quantity.

With relationships, then, obsessions will impede our growth in and through them. We may never bear fruit, or we may with a too little, too late variety. What do we need to look at, examine and take to heart in the living of more fulfilling, personal relationships? How and what obsessions are to be recognized and dealt with?

Dependencies. Having relinquished our self in favor of our ego we can isolate ourselves in the dependent state of child-parent. Instead of doing it for ourselves we can seek to have it done for us (child) or do it for others instead of them doing what they can (parenting).

We can seek to live through another person, taking on their friends, interest, life style without developing our own. We can make someone an end in themselves, finding in them the total source of our fulfillment, our reason for living. Instead of developing both the female and male aspects of our personality, we relinquish these in favor of finding compliments. We can fail to learn how to think, act, and feel for ourselves; we can suppress our feeling, intuitive, creative or rational powers.

Power Control. This is a form of overparenting. We dominate people, use and exploit them; make them believe they are helpless without us. Deep down we are afraid and insecure to surrender this role, allowing other people to just "be," because we have failed to fully mature our adult ego and our underlying "self." Should we abandon child or parent ego states, there remains the dread of being a nothing, a nonfunctional.

Emotion. Our child and parent ego states when activated harbor our most intense feelings; emotions which give us the awareness of being alive, involved. It is easy to slip into emotional addiction; this man or woman activates my sense of security, importance, suffering, nurturing, pleasure, need to be controlled . . . so we stay in the relationship, feeding on the emotions it generates, the boredom it relieves.

Sexual Pleasure. The instinct of sex and pleasure we all have takes us beyond its limits. There is a limit, where no amount of quality of the sexual experience can satisfy a more intense hunger to relate as one self to another, to share as a person, to be known for and in one' self. How often one lingers in a relationship just for that one feeling, too obsessed by it to function on any other level save for pleasure. Relationships devoid of personal feelings are all too frequent in our lives; they keep us from growing, recovering our persons, bearing fruit. Many of us have sex with no feelings involved and when we really don't want to. We feel sex is expected because I'm a man, a woman . . . after all, isn't everyone doing it?

How many of us have found that we can talk intelligently and with a shared interest with just anyone we meet? Sex is the same. Aside from a purely physical release, we really don't relate sexually with everyone of the opposite sex we meet. Sex is found by us to be a function of person, personality, and as such not everyone "turns us on."

Our world today is a noise and diversion producer . . . TV, radio, stereo, movies, etc. Where can we hear ourselves think? Even within our heads what our parents and other people and even ourselves tells us is constantly being played in the form of a relentless flow of ideas. Yet, when we engage in such a physical activity as sex, we experience a quiet, nonverbal space of pure feeling. We use sex, at times, as a means to step out of this unwelcomed, harassing mental stimulation flow.

Plugging in, God Making. As a form of dependency, we make other people the source of all our "strokes," giving them the power of making us feel sad, happy, alive. With this attitude, our obsession takes the form of looking for Mr. or mrs. "Right." We set our standards and you'd better come up to them, Buster! It is legitimate to seek treatment as a person, in a responsible, open, honest way. But there is no perfect fit for all we want from someone. If we work at it, both people committed in their concern, then we do receive the fullness of human relationships in ways we never expected. Still, we cannot set up someone as our higher power, a god if you will. Gods have a tendency to be found with feet of clay.

Relationship Trading. With this frame of mind we are never satisfied with anyone or any relationship. Something's always missing—woe to the person who lets us know it's us who's missing, who's not really communicating, sharing, loving, committing. So, like a bee who hasn't found honey yet, we go from person to person, ever hungrier and more frustrated. The often obvious dynamic of these relationships is that we play the ego role of fathering or mothering, or being a nurtured child. Nowhere do we relate as an adult, or as a person. Nowhere could we handle it when it does happen.

Goal Behavior. This is the classic case of, "I should be married now," "I need a wife to look respectable or to get ahead," "I need the security of this relationship."We make the person and the relationship a means to an end, and instead of relating to the person, we relate to the *ideas* we have concerning our relationship with that person.

Many people express feelings of aloneness with the chaos their obsessions create, that they must be the only ones to be so helpless and immature. Actually, we all experience breakdowns in our ability to relate as one person to another. Nor it the feeling that "I am, or must be going crazy to be in such a bizarre relationship which has such a strangle hold on me," a minority viewpoint. No, we are not going crazy . . . but yes, replacing our "Self" with our egos and allowing our egos to pull us into the emotional and mental chaos, frustrations, and anxiety it excells at is a *kind* of insanity. And no one can deny that this same emotional and mental whirlpool demands most of our time and energy, denying us growth or expansion as persons, restricting our developing new interests and constructive relationships with worthwhile people, isolating our world to this one *special* person.

We really *do* have a choice in this matter, a way to go, a path and a program to work. In later chapters strategies and principles will be discussed to apply in overcoming not only relationship obsessions but all obsessions.

Five

GAMBLING, OVEREATING, WORKOHOLICS, IDENTITY, LOOKS, FADS

A basic principle in our understanding of obsessions and their function is that when the self has been unloved by others and ourself into nonexistence, the ego spins off in a multitude of directions. This spin-off away from the center of our real self is seen in the form of a whole line of obsessions from which we pick to act on. In this chapter some of our every day obsessions will be discussed.

Bear in mind that with obsessions some core traits are always present:

Insanity. A cunning, powerful, baffling mind that justifies all behavior, makes excuses for every obsessive binge. The source of our frustrations; fears, anxieties are never ourselves; it is always other people, places, things which are to blame.

Loss of Control. There is no controlling an obsession. It controls us. We are powerless, helpless over where it takes us when that irresistable urge comes upon us.

Patterns. The same patterns reoccur, repeat. If it's a certain relationship that I'm always getting into and obsessed by, then it happens again. It seems like I have no choice, like I'm a victim of fate.

Running, Escape. We are always on the run from unwanted, unpleasant feelings, ideas, situations, people. These maufacture feelings cause us to live in a helpless sense of frustration ... There really is no safe place to go.

Making it Better. People, places, things, this feeling or that, will satisfy us, fill up the emptiness and release our anxiety.

What would our more common obsessive personalities tell us about themselves if we listened in on what their inner workings are telling them?

THE OVEREATER

PHILIP: So what you are saying is you saw that even death was not an answer?

ANDREA: I knew that wasn't an answer either and I went from February to October and I didn't drink or use any drugs, but I ate compulsively. I weighed 112 pounds when I left the hospital in February and when I came to the program of Overeaters in October of that year I weighed 178 pounds. I ate 24 hours a day and I couldn't face my responsibilities feelings-wise, so I did it mechanically-wise. I figured I wouldn't feel anything anymore, that I would just do what I had to do, and nobody would have any complaints. Nobody would ever know or get inside me again. I shut off; I just shut everything off. But my mind wouldn't shut off.

PHILIP: In other words, although you wanted all those feelings to stop or be numbed, in fact you couldn't arrive at that point?

ANDREA: No, not anymore. My mother told me about Overeaters Anonymous. A lady came and talked to me and I went to my first meeting and it was an AA meeting because there weren't any OA meetings then. A lady came up to me and put her hand out to me and said, "Welcome." I don't know what happened, but I didn't feel like a freak anymore. They didn't tell me to go away and they even told me they cared. I believed that the lady that was with me cared.

I've got this hollow place inside me that I'm always trying to fill up with food. A frustration, fear, or my anxiety over something triggers this inner obsession of stuffing myself to escape these harassing, unwanted feelings. Things never seem to be "right" for me; yes, I'm restless and a wanderer of sorts, always in search of the "found cure" to make it better.

Some of us are sugar-freaks, addicted to sugar; others are just food freaks in general or we pick our favorite food to over indulge in. No amount seems to satisfy, and often we'll eat to the point of sickness, throwing up and going back for more. Nor do I make the distinction of wanting rather than needing.

If I feel the obsession for food and happen to be in or near a market, I'm really dead. It's like Sherman's march to the sea all over again; anything and everything goes! And my crazy, insane mind can come up with some very convincing tales . . . eat this, it's protein, or if a little is good for you, then a whole lot must really be good! I've heard my head telling me that I'd faint if I didn't get food, and a lot of it. Everything becomes a justification for going on a binge of overeating. Let someone tell me that I shouldn't eat this or that and I release that streak of defiance in me that will take on whatever I was warned against in double fashion. But when all the smoke clears, and things are seen in perspective, it's not what I eat that's my problem, it's what's eating me!

THE GAMBLER

For me all I need to overcome my laziness and inability to do for myself or my insecurity is that one big win, the big kill. My insanity tells me that my turn will come, and it's always the next time. If I play the Stock market, then I feel I've got inside information that no one else has. Those stocks are going up because of me, something I am, think, do. There never seems to be a limit to the amount of money I could make if only . . . . Bet on anything, win everything, but never can I see what this financial irresponsibility does to me or the people I'm responsible to. I go ever deeper in debt or into savings for that Big kill. And work, who needs to work if I can do this and rake it in. Knowing things no one else knows, being able to tempt fate and win . . . what a sense of power! And should I loose, why confront that? Why call a spade a spade; I didn't really loose, I'm just learning something that I can use next time.

THE WORKOHOLIC

I get a lot out of my work; in fact, I get everything. My relationships with people are never satisfying, but with work there's always more money to be made. Nor do I really have fun or enjoy myself with hobbies, interests, sports, nature. none of those things . . . who needs them when my work gives me so much! Do I ever enjoy the money I make? No. But people think highly of me and what I do in my work. After all, isn't what we do at work who we really are?

THE GOOD LOOKER

Am I good looking or what! I can get by on my looks and get just about whatever I want. People don't get angry or confront me . . . I'm too pretty. And don't even try to compare yourself to me because we're not in the same league. So I spend all that money on clothes, cosmetics, hair styling . . . it pays off . . . doesn't it? And other people, well, they're not anything if they don't look good, really good.

IDENTITY-FADS

I am whatever I hide behind, my profession, my education, family line, what I've achieved for myself. I am what I can do, what I'm good at; I am what you think I am, what I lead you to believe I am. Feelings? I don't let them bother me or even allow them to surface that much. It's so important to me to be "in," to be doing the "right" thing, making the right scene. I get hooked on whatever happens to be the latest fad, I'm not just a vegetarian, I am *the* vegetarian. I go all the way with whatever I am "into," and if you're not into it, something's wrong with you.

Driven and controlled by an obsession doesn't leave a lot of room to grow as a person, to expand and relate to others in relationships of real sharing. There is never "enough" of whatever the obsession concerns us with. To excess is the rule. Life is seen through the glasses of our "insanity" - limited, compelling, threatening. Nowhere are we safe, nowhere are we ourselves . . . at "home."

Six

TEENAGERS—OBSESSIONS OF OUR YOUTH

ANNE: Total license is what some parents call love. Such parents don't teach any kind of responsibility. I know of a child who was allowed to lie in her bed after school and get drunk. Her parents were told by a doctor that she should be allowed to express herself in any way she wanted to. Her feeling, when we got right down to it, and it takes quite a while to get down to it, is that they didn't care about what she did. It's like what I remember my own child saying to me when I spanked him very hard, and I rarely spanked him, but he'd run across the street and I had told him over and over again not to. It was a busy, busy street. After I finished spanking him, I told him I was sorry and he said, "Oh, Mom, that's okay. I know you love me and I know you care." He wasn't but seven years old when he did that. My thoughts aren't altogether on that, but there is something there.

PHILIP: My own experience shows me there are so many teenagers and kids younger who are constantly doing things which are classified as immoral. They are constantly being judged when in fact their behavior patterns and acting up is a way of adjusting to some situation, it's a way of getting attention. It's a legitimate release expression for them. If you condemn that form of adjustment, you are condeming them totally. A basis of Christian morality is to condemn the sin but love the sinner; that distinction isn't made by many people.

ANNE: There is a sexual guilt too and our society here in the United States is sexually as sick as any society in the world. Tremendous guilts are laid on people. My own son happened to be visiting his grandparents when he was thirteen years old, and he had no interest in sex at all. But he had a girlfriend. According to him, he was not sexually awakened yet; he had no sexual drive yet. But he had a little girlfriend, and the two of them were playing records in his bedroom one afternoon. My father walked in and they were laying on their stomachs together on the bed listening to the records. They weren't even that close together. My father kicked the little girl out. My son is 22 years old and its only been in the last year or so that he's gotten over that guilt about sex. He didn't even know what he was being accused of. This is not an unusual case.

One of the most damaging things so many parents do is to condemn their children for doing what they see their parents doing all the time. little things, that are seemingly unimportant at the time they take place. A parent tells a child not to lie. It's a sin to lie and if they catch their children in a lie, a human, natural thing, they make a great deal about it. Yet the parents think nothing of the child answering the telephone and telling the child, "Tell them I'm not here." I've had that example told to me by many kids. You know, my mother always tells me that I'm a liar. Yet, she lies all the time. That kind of thing is very damaging, and we find it everywhere. That's one of the kids' chief complaints; the example they give us is that she doesn't know what she wants. She says one thing and does another. That's another thing that we do here. We try very hard to walk like we talk. We always try very hard to do what we say we are going to do.

PHILIP: Say what you mean and mean what you say. I'm also reminded of the fact that parents, not just as parents but as human beings living in our particular society, wouldn't want to take responsibility for some of their actions, acknowledging what they do because they themselves have judged themselves and in turn been judged by people and their parents. They lay that same type of guilt and judgments on their own kids. The easy way around that for them is to merely classify something as being moral, immoral, good or evil. Therefore, in a certain sense, they escape responsibility for them. All they do is point out what other people are doing.

ANNE: Do you like your life? How do you feel about your life? Do you like the way things are? These questions I direct to teenagers to find out where they're at.

PHILIP: Again, these are teenagers that you are talking with.

ANNE: Yes. Do you like your life? Then I listen to their answer and I ask how many of you use drugs? How many of you drink? And I listen to their answers. I say those of you who are happy with the way you are living and satisfied with your life and the way it is, I wouldn't presume to tell you any differently. If you like the way things are, then fine. If you don't, I have some suggestions. I do that with people when I go into jails, when I go into a school. I am not here to tell you about the evils of drugs and alcohol. I'm not here to tell you that you should change your life and live differently, that's your business. What I'm here to say is that if you like what you got, you like the way your life is, fine. Don't listen to me. If you don't, if you'd like something different, then I will tell you about something different. That's the approach that I use not only with kids but with adults, too.

PHILIP: Is there any difference between a teenager and an adult alcoholic in terms of coming to the point of seeing that they are suffering, admitting the problem,and wanting to do something about it?

ANNE: Oh, yes. The adult has built up an awful lot of layers, defenses, and totally erroneous ideas about themselves and how to operate. A youngster in trouble is much more approachable, although on the surface they don't seem to be. You have much less bullshit to wade through.

PHILIP: I remember one time I substituted in a class, I think they were sophomores; about fifteen or sixteen year olds, and I went down the list of ten points on mental health, mental hygiene, the same ten points on that tape that we listened to before. After I reached the eighth or ninth point, I noticed some of the kids in the class were crying. The tape was being played, there was no heavy thing about it. But it hit home.

ANNE: With an adult there are layers and layers of rationalizations and bullshit to wade through. They are also stronger. They have been dealing with their pain a lot longer. They have a lot more defenses. On the surface, a teenager is harder to reach because they are more out front hostile and their defenses are more apparent. To a counselor or a therapist who perhaps is not totally sure of himself or sure of his ground, they might appear harder to reach. But they really are not. It always amazes me that people are afraid of teenagers; you can crack through a teenager's defense in nothing flat. With just one question, or any one of a number of questions, such as what are you afraid of?

Immediately you get something. With an adult, you have to use a more subtle approach, go slower. The recovery is a little more hectic for a teenager, simply because they are younger or simply less educated as far as understanding words and so on. Teenagers also have a tendency to be more out of touch with their feelings because they haven't been dealing with them that long.

PHILIP: Does that also mean they are not aware of their feelings or they just don't know the words to label those feelings?

ANNE: Both can be true. I have a girl here who is not lying. It is obvious to everyone that is around her for five minutes she is afraid. But when she tells me that she is not afraid, she believes that. She is not lying, she's not trying to cover up fear. She is totally convinced she isn't afraid. She just hates everbody and is deeply angry with everbody. Just once in a long while, with a positve look on her face now that we are talking more often, she asks is that fear, does that mean I'm afraid? She doesn't know the meaning of fear because she's covered fear with anger for so long. Many teenagers are very much out of touch with their feelings, and don't have the right words to describe their feelings.

PHILIP: Do you believe that most teenage alcoholics come from homes where one or both parents have a drinking problem? Or do you think teenage alcoholism can be an isolated experience?

ANDREA: I don't know. I really haven't looked at the statistics. I've seen kids from rich families whose parents don't drink but still are very neurotic. I've seen kids of hard working parents trying to take care of them, and they're alcoholics and addicts. Why is my sister normal? She came from the same kind of environment that I did. I don't know.

PHILIP: In other words, you really don't believe there is any real environmental cause for alcoholism?

ANDREA: I guess I don't.

PHILIP: Then you are saying there really is nothing that can be said to parents whose sons and daughters are alcoholics?

ANDREA: No, I'm not saying that. Of course we have to say unconditional love is a fact and the broken home and parents as models are a factor.

PHILIP: What would you suggest to parents of a teenage alcoholic to point a way out, anything you think they need to know and do?

ANDREA: First of all, I'd ask them why they are allowing the kid to run their home because that's what's happening with an alcoholic or an addict. They run the home. What is the parent afraid of? They obviously are scared of the kid. They feel so guilty that they won't make the kid responsible for his own actions. The kid goes out and gets in trouble with the law and they pull him out of jail. The kid put himself in the position, he ought to do his time in jail. That's the way I feel. I don't think jails are any good but I think that's part of a kid's experience. I don't think parents have the right to cheat a kid out of his own experiences. If Johnny goes and breaks a window, Mommy goes and pays for it. Bullshit! The kid ought to earn the money to pay for the window and put it in himself . . . and go make the apology for doing what he did. Kids constantly aren't made to be responsible for their own actions. The parents say, well, we broke up, the environment is bad, well Johnny's lived in a slum. So big deal! A whole bunch of people live in the slums and aren't doing the rotten things they're doing. It's being responsible for your own actions. It's like finding your own sanity. Once parents start seeing it isn't all their fault, they quit letting the kid push the "guilt" button. What does the kid do? He stops because he not getting the reactions anymore. He's not running the family anymore. Everytime I talk to a parent they say, "I can't kick Johnny out." The best thing that ever happened to any of us is when the string is cut and the parents say we've had it up to our eyeballs. Pack it and take it down the road. And then they come up with "but he's a juvenile, I'm responsible." Bullshit! The kid is responsible for his own actions. If the kid has been mistreated and battered around like most of us have been, the kid is still going to have to be responsible for his own actions and the parents will have to be responsible for their own actions. You can't let a kid run the house. Parents must be in charge.

PHILIP: But how are we going to teach responsibility and unconditional love to parents?

ANDREA: They have all kinds of programs today and they all are the same twelve steps. All of them. The words have just been changed a little, that's all. You turn your life and your will over to the care of God and you write it all down on a piece of paper. You tell another human being, ask God to remove it, and you put all that into action. You make amends and every day on a daily basis you check yourself out. You pray and you meditate and you go out and share with another human being whether he is an alcoholic or juvenile delinquent, or prostitute anonymous, or parents anonymous, or whatever.

PHILIP: Human Beings Anonymous.

ANDREA: I think we all need something. It gets back to being an alcoholic and an addict. I don't know what I would have done out there with those feelings, those desperate lonely feelings. That's an old trite saying, what's it all about? What am I here for? What am I doing to justify my existence on earth? Having a baby? Big deal! A whole bunch of women have babies. It's what I did with them that counted, and I didn't do very well with them. Today it's better.

PHILIP: What would you say to teenagers who are either to the point of almost becoming or actually have become an alcoholic?

ANDREA: I'd ask them if they wanted help, and if they did I would share my experiences with them. If they don't, I'd tell them to get it off, hit bottom and hopefully make it back. You will make it to some kind of program for some help. Ididn'thave the audacity to take that experience from another human being.

PHILIP: What have you found out about teenagers you have talked to?

ANDREA: Just that they are defending their right to use drugs and that they know that I know it's more than just a feeling. There are a couple of kids that stand out in mind that are always asking what is wrong with marijuana. I throw the question back to them and make them answer it or think about it and they don't like me for that. They're just the same was as I was in high school. Smart asses. And the kids that are really interested, the kids that have questions, are not into drugs. A couple of them have found help through finding Jesus. The ones that are in most trouble are the ones that don't want to listen. They hide behind magazines and peek out periodically. You know they're hearing you. You know you're getting through. The only other thing I know is that I'm not intimidated by them. They don't scare me anymore. I know I have an answer, I know what is real.

Having shared, through teaching and counseling, with teenagers during the past fifteen years I am somewhat awed at times at teenager "survival." At no time in our lives are our emotions more chaotic, sensitive, intense; like a great pendulum, moods come over us during those years and quickly swing away.

The shift from self to ego gives rise to our obsessions springing up like so many weeds. If parents played a particularly strong parent-ego role during our formative years, readily defining who we should be and what we should not do; if being accepted, loved, understood and let alone was dependent on your performance, how "good" or how good at something we were; whether we were attractive, bright, witty, and acceptable to your parents' friends or your own peers; then this combination of overprotectiveness, dominance, possessiveness or its opposite, the teenager being able to control and boss his parents, leaves us squarely in our ego.

As we gradually shift away from our child ego we should be moving into activating and using our adult ego. But for many this "adulthood" is delayed, postponed, or cancelled completely. We may not be allowed or encouraged to take the responsibility for ourselves, due to our overprotective, I'll-give-you-everything-parents. We are in a sense kept a child, made to feel dependent. Yet, there is a deeper reality. No one is "made" to be something, to remain a child in a young person's body. We choose to do so. Our dependent child, in a sense "insane" ego, presents the illusion that as long as we're in our parents' house we cannot be our real self—a nice, neat, packaged rationalization; a cop out.

I recall being sixteen and having had my first real run-in with a full day's work for a full day's pay. I got up at 4 AM, went out into the fields miles from home to pick grapes in 115 degree heat with a hard-nosed woman straw boss. The mosquitoes were biting and the interval between rest breaks seemed forever. When I came home that evening I flatly protested to my mother, "To hell with this work bit. I'm not going out there again. I'll look for a better job." She took me aside, looked me square in the eyes and said, "Son, it doesn't get any easier. You either work or starve. It's something you've got to learn, something you *can* learn to enjoy with the proper attitude." I thought about it and instead of running from this first real adult task, I accepted it and returned to work the next day. Everyone who ever comes into man/woman or personhood must make such decisions. You've got a choice; you can be yourself, choose your newly emerging adult ego, and learn something totally valuable about responsibility to and for yourself . . . or remain a child.

Sometimes we seek to live our lives through our parents, people pleasing them, going along with their values and goals instead of carving out our own. It's like seeing a youngster in a pool showing off to his parents that he can do this or that new dive . . . and please look at me and applaud. Our ego can be obsessed with approval oriented behavior and instead of living and deciding about things to satisfy ourselves, we live and act to satisfy others . . . this includes our peer group, those we run with whose approval we seek.

Another dynamic is that going from the teens into adulthood usually means expending a great deal of energy to do and accomplish those skills which will insure success as adults. You go from playing to working. And in this society that often means goal attaining, behavior achieving and success striving, being "someone," and securing our place in the sun. There is nothing wrong with this as long as the ego *serves* the person, our self through all this. If not, then this necessary development of our ego takes over; the *ideas* of success, status and security become "real" . . . and obsessive.

And let's not forget the *pain* of meeting the whole world head on, or so it seems to us at the time. Many of us still want to be taken care of, sticking to our child ego, holding on to apron strings and parents' financial support. This takes the form of early marriage so that a wife will take care of us or a husband will . . . in search for mommy and daddy all over again. Perhaps we run off to college and hide behind the doors of this most "acceptable" institution, even receiving praise for you noble efforts. For some, college is another parent.

If you have taken the opposite alternatives, you become a parent, dominating people in your relationships, always knowing what's best, making sure everyone and everything is OK . . . I'll take care of you! Either way you remain in your ego; the self remains buried.

And that's not all that gets covered up. If parents remain in their parent-ego roles, instead of stepping out and being human, a person and friend; if your parents give love on condition of performance, if this or that, then your *feelings* remained locked away. Feelings don't like being covered up for long either. Yet, year after year some parents lay so many trips on their kids—threatening, bribing, pawning them off, making them feel guilty of "no respect" if they vent their feelings. Yes, there's going to be some long stored hostilities that come up in the form of defiance, rebellion, anger; our real self and our adult ego is seeking to be heard from. If we keep them and these feelings of ours under cover, then we learn those most painful of teenage feelings—lonliness, depression, insecurity, self-pity.

All during this same time period you're trying to be accepted by your peers. So you play follow-the-leader, or go along with what everyone else is thinking or doing. And it never works because you've go to be the one to feel, live, *own* your life and its happiness and satisfaction. No one can reunite your self and ego, or relocate your self for you.

With all this upheaval going on, our egos changing over from child to adult, or child to parent, or using all our energy to stay entrenched where we are; with this chaos producing emotional stroms within us, isolating ourselves away from people and into our own despairing anguish and self-pity, we find it open season to develop our obsessions. And teenagers are obvious about this.

Stuck on yourself. This is just plain old self-centeredness, I'm the best, the prettiest or the ugliest or the shyest. We *can* develop *negative* obsessions like a constant preoccupation with I'm a failure or a loser role.

Sex. What a pleasurable way to remain a child. Compulsive obsessive masturbation is often a daily occurrence with teens. It is a "reward" for escaping unpleasant feelings and painful failures, and it is experienced as having total control over the individual. Or it is the dominating-drawing card why men and women get together. As such it doesn't leave a lot of room for personal growth.

Performance. A carry over from childhood, the teen can be totally obsessed on how good he does things or *that* he can do things. Success in something is often carried to extremes and the teenager identifies himself solely in terms of his accomplishments.

Blame. With this obsession the young person fails to take any responsibility for his own felt inadequacies; rather the blame for his feelings, depressions, failures become other people, a girlfriend or boyfriend . . . but especially the parents.

Alcohol/Drugs. This is the beginning for the later stages of total alcoholism. Teenagers in a recent Gallop poll, identified drinking and drugs as their number one concern. The problem *is* epidemic.

Emotions. Like adults, teenagers can get totally wrapped up in a given feeling . . . guilt, anger, fear, etc. This isolates, constricts and retards all growth at the level where such obsessions begin. Hence in a person's 30's or 40's after they emerge from therapy working with their emotional obsessions, they find themselves at the emotional maturity level of a teenager or younger . . . depending when the obsession "took-over."

Time. Am I as mature as I feel I ought to be; what about my miserable childhood; my uncertain adulthood? Am I as grown up as everyone else, how do I compare? Will I get married soon, get that job I want, will I be a success after college? What is my date Friday night going to be like?

People-Places-Things. The most pressing people obsession is oneself, followed closely by the young man or woman in our life. A place may be his pad, or one's favorite escape spot; things include cars, stereo's (music and getting 'lost' in it), a favorite item of clothing.

Parents can lose themselves in "parenting," the role and identity of raising children. What about your own life, that unique expression of who you are, want, desire, value, esteem? Are you afraid to let go of the teenage son, daughter because you have no adult ego and inner self, your own person from which to live?

It is crucial that the young person begins moving away from the roles he plays, the child ego and becomes decision oriented; making those choices which will both define who he really is and insure some real measure of happiness and well being as an adult. In an obsessed state of mind, such decisions are not possible.

Seven

BOTTOMING OUT . . . AND OTHER WAYS WE HAVE TRIED

Those of us who have known the anguish and helplessness of being controlled by our obsessions know too that final pit of despair, the bottom lines in our life. For many, this total suffering may necessitate suicide, a final solution to our mental and emotional chaos. Should this be our option, then we will be killing a self we yet don't know. It would be a classic case of mistaken identity, the wrong person, a person yet undiscovered. For there is a self that we are which the confusion of our insanity and raging feelings clouds over and buries. There is a "someone" within yearning to get out, to be heard, to decide for life. Our egos present to us the illusion of our individuality; we being a solid, substantial being living a life of sheer desperation. I protest. The illusion is just that, founded on a false sense of reality where ideas and feelings appear real and the mechanism of our ego presents itself as a true "being." There is no "person" in our ego. The true "doer," "thinker," "feeler" . . . self; a witness yet unheard from.

For each of us there is a different bottom, our own unique point of no return. But it seems that all of us share in common a final stopping point where we "just can't take any more of this." We grow weary of battling, running, cowering, despairing, relying totally and completely on ourselves to pull us out ot this "mess." And nothing seems to work, no solutions do it for us. Our lives *are* entirely unmanageable. We don't like this feeling of being controlled by the dark unseen force of our obsessions.

Yet our minds suggest answers, remedies. If only we "knew" more about our problem, its processes and dynamics. What are the answers to our thousand why's? What is the psychology behind all this? These answers, a further *idea* manufacturing and hence an ego activity, is not good enough. Answers do not lie in "answers." Many of us seek the new fads of marathons, encounter week-ends, and other creations of psychologists to explore feelings, meet our real underlying natures, unveil our inner selves. These, too, do not work for the obsessed individual . . . feelings, we have plenty of! Hidden motives . . . brother, you wouldn't want to know them! What we need is something to remedy and make right our emotions and ideas at the very place and in the very process where they are created. Our search is for a total recipe, not just the frosting; for a map to be a guide out of our desert-like existences. Solutions remaining on emotional and intellectual levels alone are to no avail . . . they just don't work.

So what does? And how do we get there? And once our obsessions are manageable or even non-existent, what then? For it was fear that reduced us to the depths; fear of ourselves, of others, of life. Won't this fear and what gave rise to its inception still be within? And if we really have covered up countless resentments, hostilities, inadequacies, defects of character and plain foolishness, who wants to face all that! OK, so we'll have to face the music, confront ourselves for what we really are . . . how? And still, after all that . . . where do we go from there?

I don't know about you, but I've grown weary of presenting the problem. We've gone as far as this writer wants to go. Let's get into some workable recipes, get all the necessary ingredients and cook something we can "live" with, not just sniffing around the stove but really eating some solid food, something we so desperately need to stick to our "inners."

Eight

WE SPIRITUAL BEINGS

The very popular "Star Wars" movie had in it a reference to "The Force" and describes it as that flow of energy through all living things, uniting the universe into a concious whole. Fundamental truths sometimes emanate from the powerful media of film and television. People who saw "Star Wars" were all of one "spirit," and I felt the awareness and joy of each other when reference was made to "The Force . . . may the Force be with you."

We too often fail to live in this deepest and most real presence, we fail to celebrate our *true* nature . . . we spiritual beings. This conciousness, this Self, our "self" is not something "out there." We cannot read and understand it into existence and activity; buy it or will it into being. It's always there, whether we are aware of it or not. It is our place "within," or as Anna in the book *Mr. God this is Anna* would say, "I am in my middle."

It is our spiritual self, our person, as a part of the universal self, the whole of God that knows itself to be "alive," free, happy; that knows its true identity as love, bliss, unity, joy. It is the attainment of what is already there. When we replace our "self" with ego, then our suffering and emptiness begins. We need *fulfillment* , this need, those wants and desires taken care of which leaves us miserable when they are not. And even when they are, the satisfaction fades quickly . . . on to the next satisfaction seeking moment! Obsessions can then become a way of . . . life? No, not life . . . survival.

And our spirits, our persons are not ideas and feelings. That is why no amount of reading, intellectual discussion or debate will put us in touch with our "spirits." It would be like trying to mix fire and water.

Psychology often deals with the ego in the West. On that permise, psychology, too, can do nothing to bring us to "spirit consciousness." Even in therapy, there is a real limit that any honest therapist knows . . . there is a line of resistance beyond which no *outside* agency, i.e., the therapist, can affect change. Movement towards the spirit, which is really nothing more than being who we really are, is an inside job.

Many of us are living lives in which we feel victimized, prisoners within ourselves, unhappy, unproductive, failing here and there, hoping tomorrow doesn't come. But none of us has to continue with that kind of a life.

Let's set the record straight. The spiritual life is not necessarily the "religious" life. Religion can be a cultural, human expression, a form, a set of ideas and beliefs. Religion can be a structure, a framework, an institution, a set of rituals, songs, prayers. It can take the form of do this and don't do that, of fears and guilt and punishment. The life of the spirit, of person, is one of love, joy, freedom, peace. Sometimes spiritual, personal beings inhabit and live within the framework of "religion" . . . but they and everyone around them know they *live* the difference and wear the cloak of religion loosely.

Anne: If you look at what's happening in our society today, and not just in this country, but all over the world, there is a great shift now toward meditation . . . it's a kind of therapy. Transcendental meditation, yoga, all these things in the last twenty years have grown in interest. People are digging into all kinds of Eastern things. It's a natural result of trying to find a sense of self. We are also becoming more aware. You see adults who have been great successes. There is a commune in Germany, I can't think of the name, that's made up of young adults and all of them successful, well-educated, intelligent people who by all society's standards are successful as human beings. But they have come to a place in their life where they are empty, where the success, the acolades . . . and all these things are not getting it. They enter this community for two years. They drop out of what they were doing and they enter this community to find whatever it is that is missing. And there is a waiting list as long as your arm. There are doctors, lawyers, politicians, all kinds of people who have been success-oriented. This is what makes you a good person. They have done all those things and they've come to a place in life where, "what's the matter?" And they go and search for it. There are such communes and communites all over the world now. There is a tremendous search for the self, tremendous search for a different value system everywhere. It's not just with obessive-compulsive people. I think obsessive-compulsive people are more painfully aware."

"And more in this country, I think, than in most other countries. Part of the reason, I think is that everyone is looking for the Big Answer. I've talked to some who have gone into these different therapies and self-help who find out an awful lot about themselves. They are really turned on by all these new things they find out and then . . . Okay, so now I know, so what? The emptiness is still there. I'm still not comfortable, my obsessions are still the same, and why? Here again, this is the only "what" statement that I'll make, but I flatly believe it so. It's for every human being, not just the addict or alcoholic, the obsessive-compulsive. *The answer is spiritual.* It must be; however you conceive God to be, the answer is the spiritual. We find a sense of self, then what do you do? It's almost like phases.

During our rap session last night I was writing down the phases. There is another recovery house that has phases and I thought about what would our phases here be. It's almost like step one, step two, step three. We come to a place in life where we are washed up, whether its mentally, physically, materially; we are failures, we are bankrupt. Our lives aren't working. Whatever we are into we break out into a rash of alcoholism, or drug addiction, or whatever. We are failures, we are washed out. We ask for help and are given some help which is usually in the realm of self-awareness, finding out why. Okay, so we find out why. We kind of come to a little bit. Something is wrong. My life is a failure. Nothing is working. Why, why, why? We find therapy and people begin to tell us why. We can use such therapy here; we can use T. A., we can use E. S. T., all kinds of different things. Self-awreness; we find out why. We get very excited discovering all these new things about ourselves, some of them not so neat, but at least they are answers to why. And then we have an expectation. If we can just find out "why," everything is going to be alright. We find out why and everything is *not* alright because its still going on. And then the next thing we come to is what can we do? Well, there are methods. Some of us use a nonspiritual method, say psychiatry, psychology, or a transcendental analysis. Some of those things get better and then we come to a time, okay, so I'm not doing that anymore. Now I'm better but I'm still empty. And that's when we come to a place in our lives where there has to be a spiritual awakening. This is what I see. There has to come a time when we have to have some kind of spiritual experience."

Philip: I have often looked at this process of coming to self-awareness, as an emphasis on answering the question "why?" I have felt there could be no solution in that because I have always believed that one of the functions of the ego is the mind, the inquiring mind, the mind asking that question "why?" Not the self. The self already knows the "answer" as a solution still beyond some sort of intellectual construct. This process you were talking about, when you get to the last stage, the total necessity for a spiritual transformation, what you actually discover is that we are aware of a person, a being a self, another self, and its not only our self. Perhaps this is where the self gets its own knowledge from. Self meeting self. If we are going to meet another self, call it the Devine Being, the Deity, the High Power of God, we are going to meet another self, through self meeting self. And that is where we get our confirmation that we are okay finally."

ANNE: "I feel that because of this hunger that isgoing on all over the world, an awful lot of what we call cults are rising to feed this hunger. We come to the point in our lives where we feel we need something in the spiritual area, and there are all these people to feed it. I believe a true spiritual awakening, and the only effective one, has to be a personal spiritual experience between you and your personal higher power, whatever you conceive it to be. Young kids, especially, are going through the cult things which feed them and demand performance and lay more guilt on them when they can't perform up to the standards set. Eventually, many young people go through to the other side and find out what we stress here so strongly - your spiritual experience must be intensely personal. You and your God must accomplish this. One of the things that I try very hard not to do is to try to lay my concept on anybody else. I'll help kids through all these stages; the awareness, the awakening, the awakening that you need help, the awareness of what your problems are. All these things I'll help with. But when we come to the spiritual thing, I'll back off and say now its up to you. They don't like that. And the obsessive-compulsive personality never likes that. They want somebody to do it for them. When I tell them, alright its up to you and your God, you deal with your God, they don't like that."

PHILIP: What a lot of groups, cults, the so called-isms and -ologies of our culture do is to institiutionalize "the" answer, their answer. It becomes a tapestry. You play allegiance to the intellectual solution, too often to the theatrics of it, and you get further caught up in it. I believe God doesn't have a concept of days, like Sundays and Mondays and what have you. Actually, that is only a human construct. But I think the same type of thing is being done on all levels of our psyche everywhere. I really laugh at these so called sex surveys that have become best sellers. People actually need to be validated by someone else as to their sex lives. Well, the national average is three times a week. maybe I'll try to beat that record to prove that I'm better than the rest of us. That, I think again, is just an example. We are institutionalizing every type of answer that we come up with when its something within ourselves that has to take place. And that's a very lonely place to be when you haven't walked that road before."

ANNE: "A lot of people at the meeting I had last weekend, took exception to it. One of the questions, in the question-answer period, was, "How do I determine the difference between my needs and wants?" The statement I made as an alcoholic was I need something to eat, a place to sleep. That's all I need. Everything else is a want. There was a lot of flack about this. Everytime someone said you need so and so, I'd say no I don't need that to survive. I don't need that except for my own personal comfort, emotional, mental, or spiritual. I need a place to sleep, something to eat and the program of Alcoholics Anonymous . That's all I need."

PHILIP: "I'm reminded of Herman Hesse's Siddartha. He was asked, "What can you do?" And he replied, "I can work, I can pray, and I can wait."

ANNE: "I was talking to an older person at that same meeting and they were saying that they needed personal satisfaction, work to do, all these things. It's like that old thing, "love and do what you will." People worry about, "Am I doing the right thing, am I treating a person the right way?" All these things. We need a way of life, a philosophy of life, something to eat, a place to sleep. Everything else counts as a result of those three needs being fulfilled. If we have a personal philosophy of life that works, and is constructive and our fulfillment, our love relationships all count as a result of that. It's like in the Bible. It states as succinctly as any place else I have ever read it,"Seek ye first the Kingdom of God and all these things will be added." So often the majority of people live as if they were saying, "I'll seek all these things first and after I get all these things, then I can seek God." If I have a nice place to live and a husband or love mate, and if I'm secure, then I can take time to sit down and seek God. That's how we live. If we seek first a spiritual path, all these things come as a result of this. That's a reason why they feel empty."

I remember when I first started on this particular program that I live. There was never anything that I found within the program that made any sense to me. I think someone would say, "well, do this," and I'd answer "That is totally unrelated to the problem. What's that go to do with what I'm feeling?" That is true of any program, to have someone say, "well, try this." I experienced something personally that showed me. I was learning how to sew for the first time in my life. I had a pattern. I didn't understand any of what they were telling me. I just did what I was told to do. The inner facing of that and the outer facing of this, and sew these two things together. I didn't know what I was doing, I just did what I was told. I didn't know what I was doing had anything to do with a pair of pants I was trying to make. I simply followed the directions and when I got through I had a pair of pants. They fit and I thought to myself, that is exactly the way it is with any program. You do these things and you really don't *understand* what you are doing while you are doing it, until you see the end results. That's the way it is, with a whole lot of things. We question and wonder. We don't understand what this has to do with that, and you can't know if something works unless you *do* it.

PHILIP: We really are preoccupied in this country with knowing the underlying reasons behind things instead of the thing itself, the actual doing of the thing from which the result comes. When you cook certain things, the flavor and the chemistry involved comes out perfect. It tastes good. Everything is balanced. It is the same thing with the spiritual life, with putting your life together. *If* you do these things, then *this* will happen. And yet we really get locked up on the first level, the first stage. We spend days and months and years of our life exploring "why" instead of doing anything about it.

ANNE: I had to learn with my own life. I have learned the why in retrospect, always. I spent years in s analyzation trying to find out the why. Finally, I had to come to the point in my own life where not only did I ask why, but what can I do? After I *do* something about it, the knowledge of why it was always comes. It's always in retrospect. I never understand myself.

My father-in-law lives the essence of what all of us have scurried, scratched, and clawed to find. He is an absolute love. He is a loving human being. He came right out of the hills and from where he came, to where he is, is a long way. He spent 50 years on one job and in all that time he lost two weeks from work due to illness. He worked the soil, worked in a mill, raised his children. He's known throughout that little community. Anytime anybody needs help, he is there . . . takes baskets of fruit to all the workers down on his farm. He goes to all the funerals of everybody in town; he's never missed a funeral. He reads the obituaries in the newspaper and he's at the funerals. He takes food to the family and he is a "good" Christian but never talks about it I have never heard him criticize anybody, never heard him judge anybody. The only thing I've ever heard him say was when somebody asked him about what he thought about so-and-so marrying so-and-so. He said, in that quiet slow way of his, "Well, I think they both got about exactly what they deserve." And that was his total comment. But he lived what everyone strives to find out. He lives in the answer.

PHILIP: There are people doing it. But theirs is not the glamorous life. Theirs is not an answer that people are looking for on the surface. Theirs is the answer that people need to find, but theirs is not the answer that people are looking for. They figure if I'm coming from a point of strength, ego, status, family, position, culture, refinement, good looks, whatever, I can manipulate things based on these little limited things that I've got in my ego. But you can't do a damn thing when it comes down to the question of whether you "live" or not. Then you face yourself and there is nothing else you can resort to. Either you do or you don't and you're going to have to do a lot of work to get to the point where you "do." The world is sorely in need. I recall a story in *Reader's Digest*, where there was a black teacher in this hilltop town in one of the southern states. One of his pupils was a white fellow who eventually went into the Air Force. He left town at 18, joined the Air Force, and traveled all over for about ten years. He found out that the black teacher had died. He came to the funeral in this town of about 400 people. He was buried at the hilltop cemetery. What was so incredible was that when he got to the top of this hill he saw more than 20,000 people coming up the hill to this man's funeral! More people that two countries put together. And he couldn't believe it. Where were all these people coming from, why are they coming? Because this black teacher had merely shown a lot of understanding and love for thirty or more years laboring as a teacher there. Before he died, this fellow had a chance to come back and talk to him. The teacher asked him if he were happy in what he was doing in the Air Force. He answered, "Well, I travel a lot." "Are you happy?" "Frankly, I'm not; I haven't found myself." The teacher said, "You know there is an awful lot of work to *do* in this town and the surrounding area." Well, after the teacher's death this fellow got out of the Air Force, got a teaching credential, and took the man's place. He was writing the story after the event. He found that you are always needed. There is always work to be done. You never have to worry about boredom, you never have to worry about self-centeredness. There are four growing seasons out of the year instead of one, and things to be reaped. I learned this lesson with a woman I once knew. I thought she was an alcoholic, a prostitute. She had used drugs and alcohol. But regardless of that, the real lesson I had to relearn again with her was really unconditional love. She wrote me a letter not too long ago saying she was happy. She had found a good man that was capable of sharing with her and she with him. I felt so good about it. I really feel that whatever ego I had in terms of our relationship, I've grown through it. I'm hoping possible she could see God in her life. I really see that as freedom. That is where freedom lies. The freedom to love is the ultimate freedom. Everything can flow from that one experience. Spiritual, yes. It really embodies the entire person. I think that sometimes in my life I've had to see that the body is part of that expression, too. That is probably the point in Christianity that is one of the shakiest in terms of making that marriage between body and soul. Constantly, people love through their bodies. It's not just a personal feeling. It's not a psycho-metaphysical experience. It is when you hug somebody, when you kiss somebody, when you dry their tears. Numbers and numbers of things. Feed them, clothe them. It's all through the body to the soul.

ANDREA: We've got to stand up and speak our own truth. If we don't, we just wither and die. We pass out of this life not learning anything. It's been a fruitless life. Maybe that again is too idealistic and putting a blanket on everybody. I see myself doing that. That isn't good enough for me anymore. Somehow I'm powerless to stop growing. There's something inside me that says, "no," you will not stop. You are going to continue growing no matter what. I made a decision to grow up. I made a commitment to my God and to myself that I was going to grow up, and that growing process is getting back to my God.

So let we, the obsessed, or anyone else in search of their true self, their real "home," real living, turn to the life of the spirit, of being who we really are . . . a person. There is a time, a readiness when this turning and spiritual awakening comes. For each it is different, but for *all*, the self-(ego) will, solid, separate, fighting against the world type of individual insanity and anguish must first cease. We've got to "put down our guns," deactivate the bombs inside. Each of us chooses our life, with a lot of rope to hang ourselves. Just as our obsessions controlled us, we come to the awareness that we *can* do something about them by choosing the *real* workable options we have in following the principles, path and spirit, of the spiritual life; of living who we are, of releasing that terribly beautiful loving force within us . . . our "self."

As we begin our journey, the discovery of who we really were all along, of sweeping away the dust the ego deposited from the weathering on the statues of our egos we worshipped, a new level, a new world, a homelike place of life is revealed, the workings and fruits of the spirit unfold to us: Peace, love, freedom, responsible choices, trust, faith, joy, friendship, the celebration of ourselves, each other, *life.*

Just as being a sexual being has its steps, its path we so eagerly seek to discover and follow, so too our spirits must be allowed, given permission to do their thing; our lives come together as our persons are made whole again and our true "hearts" allowed to act upon and in life. The principles, steps and paths of action and being which follow, await our application and practice.

Nine
HUMILITY

For those of us who live in our obsessions and emotional chaos, the beginning of our spiritual path is humility. In this we admit to ourselves our helplessness in the face of our obsessions, our unbridled emotions and confused minds . . . the dominance of our ego over our self.

There is no one else left to blame for our condition, our broken or unfilled and empty lives. We have had enough, we have chased our own tails to the point of exhaustion, we have used up all manner of excuses and rationlizations

It is not easy, this first outreach for our lost self. We are not sure, being on the totally unfamiliar ground of relinquishing our self-will, the self-seeking life style of I, mine, where and how and from whom can I get my desires satisfied. This beginning is born of suffering . . . we finally admit "I hurt." Having run from ourselves and used the mechanism of gratifying our obsessions and dulling or tranquilizing our minds and feelings, we find nowhere else to go. We have painted ourselves into the corner of our own souls where there is nothing else left. The god we have made ourself topples, or the total nothingness we have thought ourselves to be still knows the despair of ceasless anguish.

As we make this acknowledgement of defeat, almost at once we begin finding relief. That outpouring of energy we used, to blame something or someone for who we are, stops. We find ourselves in a quiet, strange place. For the first time in a seeming eternity, we actually do see something as it really *is.* We see what we have become, and just how much it really does hurt. Yes, we have made our own bed; but in that awareness comes the hope that we can unmake it. For that matter, and we don't know it yet, we're in the iniital stages of actually moving not only out of our "old bedroom," but into an entirely new house!

This first spark of hope! Crucial, and yet coupled with it is the ability to see things as they really are, to see ourself as we really are. At first this will mean our negative, suffering self, all the foolishness we have made ourselves into. But the underlying "self" is just over the horizon. A self not known through the forms and labels of teacher, housewife, man, woman, Protestant, Jew, intelligent, attractive, ugly, American, Russian, etc. We see our self as "is" when our blinders have fallen away.

We feel a burden begin to relinquish itself; this being the burden of that terrible and awesome dread that we are all alone; that it's totally up to us to live our lives, we can expect help from no one, nowhere; that we are pitted against "them" and the "world," even "life" itself for our survival. Our obsessed egos would have us still believe this to be. As humility becomes a part of our search for self, we learn the falseness of these former attitudes. We discover we do have options in the spiritual life. We understand things as they are.

The key to this inauguration into the spiritual life is a willingness to take the next step, to push up and do what has to be *done.* We allow ourselves to become teachable, willing to learn who we and others really are; what life is really all about. *Seek and ye shall find.*

A final challenge rises to meet us. When we finally stop running, it becomes apparent that we are alone. It is from within ourselves that the decision to live our own life, in a responsible fashion, and in harmony with the spiritual nature we find ourselves to be, must come. No one else, no one we have ever depended upon, can do it for us. Only we can live our own life . . . only we can experience on another level we are not alone . . . there will soon exist for us a spiritual fellowship where our physical, mental, emotional, and spiritual beings will work in harmony, giving us our long sought happiness.

PHILIP: What is this spiritual transformation all about? How do we get healed?

ANDREA: For me the first thing I had to do was see that I had a problem, that it wasn't everybody else, that it wasn't society, it wasn't my mother, it wasn't my environment. *I* had the problem. I had to become teachable. I had to open my mind. All of this is not by virtue; it's hurting so damn bad. Suicide hadn't worked, drugs and alcohol quit working, compulsive overeating had not worked. Sex had not worked. Nothing had worked. When I came under the program and people told me, first of all that I had to not drink, use, or run no matter what and it would be okay, I didn't understand.

But for some reason I believed them. I don't know why. I hear people say in the program, "I saw your bright, shiny eyes and I wanted what you had." I didn't want it. I was terrified when I came into AA, absolutely terrified.. I felt as if I had just crawled from underneath the rocks, taken off my clothes, and was standing naked in front of the world. I didn't have anyone to stop the pain. I turned myself in, into AA and Overeaters Anonymous. People started saying that they did the same things I did. They started saying that God was the only answer, and I didn't want to hear that. The hair used to stand up on the back of my neck. God had rejected me and I had rejected God years before that. I didn't want to hear about that. All I could see was walking into a church. I was going to have to go to church. I was going to have someone sprinkle some ridiculous water on me. My whole feeling about sprinkling water on me was by whose authority does it make it holy? It was something to do. Going to a lot of meetings for me was something of an escape, it was something to get me out of my home. I had never been allowed out of my home. People acted like they were happy to see me. They put their arms around me and they didn't tell me I stunk, and they didn't tell me I needed a bath. They didn't say I was too fat to love. I needed that. I was so desperate, so lonely. Just the mere fact that somebody had reached out and touched me was absolutely amazing. I had been a toucher all my life, and I had been rejected so many times that I stopped looking at people, reaching out to touch people. When I stopped having anything to do with my husband, which was five years before that, I had asked him for a kiss and he said, "Not when you act like a dog that has its tail behind him." We had been married five or six years at that time and I never asked him again and I never touched him. That was it. It was all over. I couldn't open myself up to that type of humiliation again. These people didn't ask that, they didn't ask for anything. They put out their hands to me and said, "Welcome." I didn't really believe them, but something kept bringing me back. I had been married nine years with three kids to show for it. It was exciting and people just started loving me. Then they'd ask if I wanted to talk. Nobody had ever asked to hear my opinion on anything. They wanted to know what I thought about certain things as if they cared. For the first time I could see the look in their eyes. They were laughing and it was scary for me, but at the same time it was comfortable. I'd never had that. One day somebody said, "They say you're an alcoholic and an addict." Then I knew why I did the things I had done. For a long, long time I heard people say, "You weren't responsible for anything you ever did when you were drinking." Well, most of the things that I did I thought were so horrendous that I could never tell another human being I did those things even when I was stone cold, sober and without drugs. I would go insane. There was a screaming inside me for something to put the pain out. That's when I tried to drown my son. I was stone cold, clean and sober, and had been for a long time. I went bezerk that day. I'd smacked him 'cause I couldn't stand the screaming so I was determined to scare him. I blamed it on my older son. For years I couldn't tell anybody I had done it. He almost died because of it. I wasn't born with a sixpack around my waist. That wasn't what my mother wanted for me. It wasn't her fault for what I became. The only answer that my neighbor had the day I went totally bezerk and stark raving mad was to give me several tranquilizers. I took them, and it started to put the volcano out. I went on my next five year run before I came into the program. There again was my answer. The answer had been there at nine and again at twenty. When I had surgery, the answers as more chemicals. When I came into the program, they told me I no longer had to take any of that. The answers were in the big book of AA and I started reading the big book. The answers were there to all the questions I'd ever had in my whole life. The answers were in those twelve steps to recovery. I started taking them. That was the answer in the beginning but it kept mentioning God and it kept mentioning being rocketed into the fourth dimension, being reborn. We had to die, we had to admit complete defeat, and all those things. After about a year I met a lady who'd been sober about ten years at that time. She was considered by most people as totally insane. Her whole thing was doing what her heart told her to do. She explained being rocketed into the fourth dimension to me. She explained being reborn to me. She explained Karma. In truth, I didn't have any other choice because that was what I was supposed to do. That relieved the responsibilities, saying I didn't have to take respnsibility for my own actions. It relieved the guilt that I was so rotten and horrible. I didn't now have alcohol to blame. I finally saw my insanity through 11 steps. The third step had talked about prayer and meditation, turning my life and my will over to the care of God as I understood Him. In the beginning He was really punishing me. I heard people saying God was a loving God and that their God had a sense of humor to put up with them. It made sense to me, after all I had been given a second chance. I had been put in a program where a whole bunch of people were finding a different way to live. The people that I was attracted to had a spiritual way of living. I believe the whole package of life is spiritual and if I haven't got that, I don't have anything. I couldn't find it in churches because it wasn't God as *I* understood Him. It was God as *they* understood Him. I look back and he never came down with a bolt of lightning and got me. There must be something to God that is love. I started putting those beliefs and my faith into action. I started doing those things I was told I could never do, just little things and finding out it was okay on the other side. That really made me a happier person.

PHILIP: What were these little things that you did that made you happier?

ANDREA: In the beginning the thing of being programmed by society and my mother; this is a small but an important example to me. My mother told me I could never wear turtle neck sweaters nor dangling earrings because I had a short neck. When I got into the program, I bought a turtle neck sweater. That was stepping out and doing something that I feared to do because I was going against what I had been programmed to accept all my life. I found out I looked good, including the dangling earrings someone gave me. I wore them and no one laughed at me. I then decided what kind of clothes I liked to wear. I went through this stage in my sobriety where I was absolutely blatant in everything I did. I became a biker. I wore a Harley Davison patch on the back of my pants, and I was proud of myself. I was stepping out and doing things. When I cut my kids and my husband loose, I sold everything I owned and flew to Hawaii and lived there for a time. I lived off the land. I started putting into practice that God would take care of me as long as I was doing His work. His work, I didn't know what it was, but I was learning and finding out. I found His work was to carry the message. I don't believe the only message there is is A.A. I believe that the message is love, unconditional love. I just started doing little things that people told me to do—do something for another human being, and don't let them find out about it. That was a big thing because my ego got in the way. I wanted you to know what a good girl I was. I did that over and over until I had fun in trying to find things to do for people. I would sit in a group of people that I was living with and everybody was saying, well, who did such and such. I wouldn't even crack a smile. If I smiled, they'd know. I worked on not letting them know.These little things I did for others were enormous steps for a person like me who was so terrified I couldn't even drive a car when I was sober. I couldn't go into a grocery store by myself. I got my driver's license. I got my first checking account. I bought my first coat. I had never owned a coat and I stepped inside a store and decided what I wanted to wear. Those are very human things, but I was finding out my own likes and dislikes and that to me was stepping out and doing things I was terrified to do.

PHILIP: It sounds as if for the first time you were really living your own life, being your own person.

ANDREA: Yes, that's true. I became willing to accept the responsibility for my own actions. I started talking in meetings and expressing how I felt. Time and again I was put down, but I would still express my opinions. I became teachable only out of pain, sheer agony.

Ten

GOD . . . WHO?

We have acknowledged and accepted our state of living as the uncontrollable anguish that it is. A sense of openness and willingness in our search is touched upon. Almost like the unfolding of dawn a new presence comes upon us. We are asked to believe in a previous unseen power, greater than ourselves. There is a word to name this presence . . . God. But we protest. The God we have known from childhood . . . punishing, fearful, structured, a theology of beliefs. No. No, this is not God as we are now coming to reach out to, and within for. That "God" was an idea, a structure of concepts, and perhaps a punishable set of do's and don'ts.

Each of us is unique in our experiences, our lives; a different expression of consciousness and life. In this spirit of uniqueness we come to God in our own way, in the way in which God reveals himself to us as our higher power. The form of this revelation stands as minor, accidental . . . the God who reveals and is revealed, the God we come to relate to is the ultimate truth.

In this relationship we discover the loving power of God who acts within us to restore us to our original self, or our undiscovered 'person,' spirit. Our insanity caused by the ego's take-over is absolved, begins to disappear. We see we are not blind, however blurry our first visions are.

What follows in the remainder of this chapter is a sharing with you. Please, it is not meant to be "dogma" . . . it is my truth, what has given me "life" . . . what for me I have come to know as "life."

In the beginning I came to know Him; that is when my real life began. He came, this God. I've known Him through the medium of love, through the agency of another person. In His coming all former ways of thinking and feeling, of obsession and ego, began to fade and lose their hold.

Have you known a true friend, with whom the whole of your being is alive, with whom all is peace, all is accepted. This "friend"; between you is the bond of love, a joy no person can take from you. In that love and relationship you grow, come to know your true self. No judgments are rendered and any fault quickly and easily forgiven.

I came to know God in this way; a friend who cared, in a forever, unconditional way. No words can describe who I grew to know and love. With God I came to see myself like a wave upon the ocean . . . separate only in the form of being a wave, of something rising out of the water, yet totally a part of that ocean of "self." It remains for each of us to discover this personal relationship to our higher power, our God; no one else's God will do.

Above all I met God as a Friend, a person who loved me; a part of me and I a part of Him. This meeting takes place with all of me; everything I am, I own and give in this encounter. In this space between us I found my completeness.

Once, when I was nineteen, I was loved and in return loved that someone very much . . . totally. While looking upon her and sharing ourselves together my field of vision began to change. The trees, grass, sky, all began fading from view. All color and material forms disappeared. Slowly she began to "disappear" until all that was left were her eyes suspended in space and through whom I "saw" from a place within my soul and heart, her Person, her self. Soon, even "she" faded from my experience and I was left with a radiant kind of glow, but not any color we know in our material world. This "white" light filled all my senses and I came to know the person of God for me. There was total peace and love, acceptance in God's presence. And what a "presence." Within me stirred the deepest feelings of love, surrender, joy, peace; I knew who I was, and that I was complete. No words or ideas accompanied or shaped this "event." It was rather a holy or sacred birth for me, the establishment of a special love for my friend, God. I cried tears of unrestrained happiness. I knew then not life as "what was," but life as "who was."

For me the reality behind "God is love" and the episode where Moses found through the revelation of the burning bush God's identity to be "I am who I am" forms a base from which my relationship to God has grown.

God as love has a total and all encompassing love . . . unconditional. I sense that my human destiny is to be fully alive and thus cooperating with what God's will from the beginning of time has been . . . my happiness in the showing of Him in love, in His "self," His "person." This is life. And I have found Him to be everywhere. In all of nature, from the smooth flow of rose petals to the delight of rain falling from the heavens. Together we form a relationship, a dynamic friendship of "we" . . . that is, when I allow and choose this relationship, for I have found myself to be defined in this power of choice.

With God, I simply "am," things "are," in the same way that He has revealed Himself as "I am who I am." God is of the present moment, now. We need not wait for His coming or death to lead us to Him, for He truly "is." The Book of Revelations joyfully proclaims something of the wonder of His love and our relationship to Him in Revelations, Chapter 21, Verses 1-8:

> When I saw a new heaven and a new earth; for the first heaven and the first earth had passes away, and the sea was no more. And I saw the holy city, new Jerusalem, coming down out of heaven from God, prepared as a bride adorned for her husband; and I heard a great voice from the throne saying, "Behold, the dwelling of God is with men. He will dwell with them, and they shall be his people, and God himself will be with them; he will wipe away every fear from their eyes, and death shall be no more, neither shall there be mourning nor crying nor pain anymore, for the former things have passed away. And he who sat

> upon the throne said, "Behold, I make all things new." Also he said, "Write this, for these words are trustworthy and true." And he said to me, "It is done! I am the Alpha and the Omega, the beginning and the end. To the thirsty I will give water without price from the fountain of the water of life. He who conquers shall have this heritage, and I will be his God, and he shall be my son."

For God as spirit speaks to and acknowledges us, reveals Himself in the total spectrum of matter and spirit . . . for we who have searched so long and painfully, all things *are* made anew!

In this meeting of God we see that we are made in His image. We are of spirit and love; we can love and we can "know," we can "choose." We are at best, "I am who I am," living each moment now, surrendering our preoccupation with past and future; surrendering to our limiting identities of "I am . . . me, a man or woman, of this race, creed or color; of this country or that; having this intelligence, job, place in society." Persons, as we soon discover, are not defined or limited in conditional, changing ways. Rather, our true self simply "is," complete, here and now, joy.

Each of us comes to God in due season, in our own time and on our own path. Beyond the path and time He is the same for us all. Trust, acceptance, surrender, and love bring us to Him.

In the meeting of God, knowing God, living in His love, we find the core of our spiritual growth, just as we experience so much growth and life in our human friendships. There is no more room for our obsessions, the emptiness is filled. Universal self, with our self, embrace. And we begin a new life of finding that what we thought to be a search for the "wave" of our own "self," expands into an endless ocean of Love and "Self."

PHILIP: You mention this confusion you have that all of us really share. All of us are confused to a point. It's just how much do we want to admit to. What for you has been confusion.

ANDREA: As a kid we weren't allowed to talk about God in our house. I went to a lot of churches and I didn't get any answers to any of my questions. My mom was really super against God. Don't ever mention Him. At a certain point in my life, because I was told that if I did bad things I would be struck down by God or by lightning, and it didn't really happen, I checked Him off my list. He really isn't interested in me and He's ignoring me. I'm so rotten that well, forget it. I was in the seventh or eighth grade, maybe even younger at the time. When I got married and had my second child, who was born with a heart disease, my mother told me not to blame God. it was like, what are you talking about? All my life you wouldn't even let us talk about God, and everytime I went to church you got so pissed! Now you are saying don't blame God. I didn't understand.

The first thing I had to do was break through the fear of God. I was almost thirty and I was going through a very painful experience. I was pregnant, with three children, and the guy of my security had walked out the door. I was left to depend on something other than myself. I got so angry that I wanted to kill this kid. I found myself getting on my knees and saying God please save me from this anger. It was the very first time in my life that I ever felt that everything was going to be okay. The anger left and I felt warm and secure and it was alright. That was the beginning, believing that maybe there really was something else.

They talk in the big book of AA about the world of spiritual make-believe. I believe that is what I was living in. I believed that if I didn't have any money in my pocket and the car didn't have any gas, that God would put gas in the car. That's spiritual make-believe. He doesn't come out of the heavens with a gas nozzle and stick it in your car. He gives you the job to earn the money to put the gas in the car. I didn't want to do that. I was different and I was rising above that. I was fairly spiritual. Then I came down to learning about my humanness. That's where I've been ever since, learning about Andrea and her humanness. That's why I say you can't get from A to C without going through B. It has taken me all this time of not calling myself dirty names when I have a human feeling; when I get caught up in all the humanness around me. Now I see myself as going through a lot of layers of surrender and of acceptance, of learning different concepts about my God. I bet He isn't quite as personal as I thought he was. But it's all the same for everybody. You stand outside and it's raining, it's going to rain on the person that just shot somebody. And if he's standing next to me, it's going to rain on me, too. The sunshine shines on everybody, too. So my concepts have changed about my God. I call Him God today. I don't have to change the name. I feel, at times, a thing this lady referred to as the dark side of the soul. Sometimes I feel very sad inside and it has nothing to do with the outside. And there is a hunger to get closer to my God as I understand Him. I don't know at times what to do but then a book or somebody will come into my life. The thirst and hunger will subside for a while. Then I go out and do my thing. But I have to have times during the day where I'm by myself, quiet, sometimes sitting out in the middle of the desert and letting the energies of the desert come in and give me some strength back. I can't work on a constant basis of giving and giving and not receiving anything back. My cup is empty and I've got to fill it. I'm trying to be good to Andrea by taking these trips. And I'm finding all kinds of things in that world for mental stimuli, doing what I'm doing right now—speaking at schools. I love it when people ask me a question and I try to answer it and it makes my brain work. I believe that has something to do with God. God is all there is. There isn't anything else. God is it. Do you know when everything is dried up and blown away what is left? God. Nothing is important; there but getting back to my Father. I've learned that on the program, the program that I live by and not just the 12 steps. I got off into a trip two or three years ago. I started dropping out of AA because I became very self-righteous, but I still use some of those concepts today. I have to remember that I am an alcoholic and an addict and I can go flying off way out there and get lost someplace. My main objective in life is to get back to my Father. That's what all the lessons are in the end; to get back to my Father.

PHILIP: Do you see that you have a cooperative relationship with God your Father?

ANDREA: Not entirely so, no, because I still have a layer of fear.

PHILIP: But is this an ideal, at least, to get to the point where you are cooperating with God, your Father?

ANDREA: Yes. My favorite prayer is St. Francis of Assissi. I've prayed and meditated on that for eight years. That's what I want. I want to be a servant of my God and do whatever His will is and not to have all my selfish desires. But I have to become aware of that selfishness before I can get it out. That's what the program does. It makes me aware of my humanness so I can better do my God's will.

Eleven

I SURRENDER . . .UNCONDITIONALLY

With surrender, we discover we cannot simply do everything ourselves. When I was seventeen I came to know one of the profoundest and most meaningful experiences of my life. It was more than a "lesson," it was a cornerstone in the whole process of spiritual, personal growth.

I had a female friend who for almost a year sought to share with me everything about herself. Daily she would seek me out at lunch to talk, to share her concerns. At night she would call me and seek to communicate anything and everything she was feeling; I'd get phone calls, invitations to go out with her and to feed and groom her horse. So many precious moments she gave to me. Yet, like I had a heart of cement, I accepted but rarely responded from within myself.

It was the morning of New Year's that year and I spent it somberly walking the deserted streets, reflecting on our relationship. Suddenly, like an earthquake from within, a clear, sharp, unavoidable truth sprang up and presented itself for my consideration . . . "Jane loves you, Philip." It came with an intensity far stronger than words.

Slowly I began *deciding* something inside, saying a "yes" to her and the presence of her love. I began "surrendering" to her, to a love that had been growing inside of me, to "us." The experience of all this was awesome, beautiful, and I knew real release and joy for the first time . . . and a sincere love. My own awareness of all this remains distinct after all these years, for I had crossed over into a new way of living, feeling, thinking. Yet, with all the joys came the sorrow months later of saying "good-bye," of surrendering again the fulfillment this relationship had given me. It was so painful, yet so necessary. The result surprised me. I found myself still to be terribly happy and strengthened at such deep levels within myself.

If you do not know and practice the next spiritual step of

surrender, then begin. And if you do, let us share the new life we have found and celebrate its fruits.

Let us now look again at the individual we were and the person we are now beginning to grow into. Many of us found our lives deficient and wanting. We were not complete, happy, at peace or productive anywhere near our capacity. Instead, we had settled into a life-style founded around our ego and our self-seeking, self-will. Things were seen as "mine," and it was too much of "me," and "I." We had replaced "I need," with "I want," "I am" with "I have." Through our self-will we filled ourselves with pride, with the notion of ourselves having power, controlling life and others. It was survival, us against the world. I remember leaving college with the notion of "well, there's a jungle out there. I've got to hustle and compete and get ahead." The only "ahead" I ever got was a head of lettuce. I had visions of carving out my own place in the sun, my piece of the empire. In the process, we tend to dominate others, making them dependent on us or play the dependent child and get something from whatever benevolent "parents" we conned into our game.

Our self-will encouraged our cultivation of the negative virtues centered in our pride.

lust—sexual pleasure left us empty. We felt driven to always have it, to, conquer another human being; emotions of the heart were absent.

anger—frustration marked a daily way of life; frustrated at not being ourselves, of seeking always the satisfaction of our wants; of realizing all our ideas about life and our expectations of things to come "true," angry as hell at people, places, and things when our "security" failed to materialize.

laziness—we sought dependent relationships or slave-master, as the easy way out . . . sugar daddies. No responsibility was accepted, and we avoided admitting we really did not earn what we got.

greed—we could never get enough of anything to satisfy us, to make us "feel" good. The only sense of well-being we had was a material one.

fear—we were afraid of living, of doing, of getting out in the world and being a real person among real people.

self-pity/depression—we feed ourselves a steady diet of depression (anger or frustration turned against ourselves) and self-pity, that poor old me game, won't somebody pay me my due attention and side with me . . . against myself.

With the practice of our new found spiritual life, we can now go to that virtue of "surrender." Already we have admitted our true state of affairs as being hopeless, uncontrolable and unhappy doing our life "our" way. Then we moved into the assertion and belief of God's real, working existence in our lives, a God that was unique to each of us and not really "defined" by any one person's experience. We came to know God as we understood Him to be, as he revealed Himself to us in *our* life.

With surrender, we discover we cannot simply do it all at once. We find it happening in bits and pieces, a little at a time. What we must remain constant with is our willingness to surrender as we are able. It's like an apple tree growing; over several seasons and a lot of bad weather it grows fruit. Still, we must give up our old ways, our "negative virtues" . . . they have shown us no good results, they do not "work," and consequently our lives have not "worked." A key in our surrendering is the awareness that the God each of us discovers, this higher power, actually *does* care about us. How is this to be understood? For me, I came to the realization that I did not create love, friendship, beauty, person . . . God did. I felt a force of life, within life that was life. This force was personal, sought me out, and fought to express itself in and through me, all I had to do was surrender, say "yes." It was like seeing a flower grow into bloom and see that some "beautiful life force" sought to express itself. I was shown this through the love and friendship of people . . . and how happy I was when these expressions of a caring Life came into my life. So I could *trust* this God I was growing into a relationship with, I could turn my life and my will over to Him . . . secure in the experience and trust of His caring. The more of my self I surrendered, the fuller within the "Self" grew. This filling up of my spirit and the actualizing of my person came out in the form of my love for others, my joy in living, a peace that followed wherever I went. Inside of me was my "home," yet the whole world also became "home."

Of course, our egos put up a battle during all this . . . when does it ever stop! I kept getting this playback of "but, if you surrender, you won't have anything," and my experiences kept showing me that "nothing" (no-thing) is ever really "mine," I really don't "have" anything so I can surrender *everything!* We can then begin this process of turning over our lives and wills to our caring God and grow to know Him.

This is not a passive process, it is quite active. We and our lives become defined and realized in a steady flow of decisions within our "selves" and not our egos. We give up worrying about our lives, their outcome, if we're going to 'get" all those things we *want,* if people are going to think all those things about us. We then begin seeing that life, *our life,* is what we do and create in it, what we allow (surrender) into our lives . . . love, friendships, joy, freedom, service, creativity, and peace. We slowly but surely realign our wills to God's will, God's will for us. We disattach and surrender all those *old* feelings and living patterns that held us back. I found that I *do* have a choice about how I feel. If I feel depressed or angry or hurt or disappointed, I simply (well, *not* so simply!) surrender those feelings and assert new ones in their place—joy, peace, etc. Try it. Next time you feel the old feelings, surrender them and *choose* instead emotions you really want.

As we surrender, we discover our lives beginning to unfold as we always really wanted them to. I searched four years after college for the job "I" wanted and a few days after I surrendered and turned my concern over to God, someone called me and offered me "the job" I had been so long looking for—Try it . . . you *will* like it! All this is inevitable if we let the life force of God into our hearts and lives. Take a look at flowers everywhere you go. In each one of them, no matter where or in what conditions they live (this is for you environmentalists who believe one's external conditions *strictly* determine you and your life), beauty is expressed . . . Life will have it's way. And Life, God, wants to have His say, if we allow Him to do His thing! And His thing is so much more totally satisfying than our thing.

I had to develop a gentle acceptance of myself as I grew towards being myself. I needed to *forgive* myself all that I had been; refrain from judging or condemning myself. I had to surrender my past after truly admitting it and accepting responsibility for having created "me" and all my frustrations. In surrendering, we seek to be what we already and all along are but never allowed ourselves to be in touch with.

In letting go, we let God do and be. And this friend of ours, this higher power of ours, this senior partner, has He not let us in on a powerful but simple secret that he is known as "I am who I am." In surrendering, we *are* letting things "be," we are *allowing* God to "be,"—and therefore to "do." Things as they really were, we as we really are (not what man's self-will and ego have made) are in and of God. Talk about ultimate *security;* we are the wave on the ocean of SELF, of God. God does take care of His "own" . . . for to deny us relationship, love, unity with Himself after we've surrendered our lives and will to Him would be to deny His very self, for how can the wave not be part of the ocean! And how can we, the living, not be part of Life!

In surrendering we disattach ourselves from our identification to ideas and feelings. We also are "I am who I am"; made in *this* likeness and image of just "being" . . . not I am a teacher, an Air Force major, woman, an American, a Democrat, a Catholic. We are self, person, unlimited by ideas and words unless we choose to be, unless we seek to act out countless roles and parts these ideas would have us play. In this kind of surrender, we find a new spontaneity, a sense of joy, of being now!

By practicing this spiritual step of surrender, we also begin clearing up confining relationships. Where once we may have been defensive, self-denying any deficiencies in us or admitting to our dependent, dominating or irresponsible, unloving ways, now we practice step one of admitting, accepting, and now surrendering those things in our relationships which hold us back from true happiness. Important, too, we ask our God to come into our relationships and be a part of, a loving, personal part.

All this is a kind of "growing up." We find ourselves at first alone before our God, but trust on our part and care on His creates a working relationship, a meaningful surrender. Insread of continuing with any real dependent ties on anyone for our growth and happiness, we surrender our Self over to the loving, creative power within, to the Life each one of us participates in. Yes, we are all equal before our God, all on the same path. We need not go to anyone else for our spiritual Self; our life is within! As Christ acknowledged that the Kingdom of God is within us, so we come to surrender to this reality. Our Self, Life, love, God . . . in and of each other . . . a Unity.

The surrender of our will and our lives does not mean, as those who fear this step would have us believe, that its all over for us now; that we've just been done away with, that there is nothing for us to do. On the contrary! We see, through surrender, that our lives have really been in just a holding pattern, a keeping away from, a holding back activity. We've not lived, we've "survived." Now this heavy burden drops from us as we seek to conform our will to God's, as we allow our higher power, the universal Self to express all that He is through us . . . and that's a *whole lot* to express. Just developing and allowing His presence to "be" (called love) among the people we know right now is a lifetimes's work, let alone through and with all those people we've yet to meet. It is not a destruction of our will and ego we are after; it is conforming and surrendering them to the dynamic interplay with God and His will. Action, challenge; you want something to grab hold of and wrestle with, you've got it!

In talking with numbers of people about the conflicts of surrendering one's obsessions and reflecting on the difficulties, several key objections are raised. We ask, "Why should I give up my obsessions . . . with drink, certain feelings, sex, this man or this woman, sugar, tobacco, money, etc. It feels *good,* it's stimulating, it's a fair remedy to boredome, it doesn't harm anyone. Obsessions are never surrendered nor even the desire and active commitment to change them begun unless at a deeper level we feel the confinement of their control over us; unless we sense the futility in them trying to make it better inside and realizing it never is. We truly must want to change, to have grown weary of unproductive living habits, relationships; people, places and things that just never brought a fulfilling peace within. "But if I surrender something which at least I can claim *some* level of satisfaction, some of the time, in favor of a 'new way,' what will I be getting? We are skeptical, fearing we will end up with nothing.

In our surrender, we do so not to a God or life force or beliefs, of dogmas and ideas; we find our God to be a power we can *relate to,* stand in relationship to, converse and share with. We do not surrender, at any time, to an idea or ideas, no matter how fancy. There is no philosophy or theology here. There is Life, the life behind all the beauty of nature, all the love and friendship and joyous sharings between persons.

Rachmoninoff, the talented and famous musician, once remarked that if he failed to practice one day, he would know the difference, two days and his wife would know the difference, three days and his audience would know the difference. So with us. Those things we fail to surrender, to turn over to God, become problems, sometimes spreading to infect greater and deeper extents of our person. Surrender *is* a daily necessity, just as breathing and eating is. At the beginning of each day we can surrender the day, its concerns and problems, our wants, desires, needs over to God. We can give of ourselves. When emotions or ideas seek to engulf or harrass us, just surrender them, give them up, release our hold on them.

These concerns can be as broad as the very themes of our lives, as was brought out in the book *Passages*. Our careers, marriages, productivity, growing old . . . all to be surrendered. They can be as direct as being able to get along with this person or that at work; as intense and personal as the quality and feelings within our love relationships. every aspect of our life, surrendered, becomes a new aspect of Our Life, we and our God's. Within ourselves we find a new kind of security, a wider base of support. Underneath all our sufferings and problems, behind all those terribly important concerns, within our very being we discover the caring support of God, our friend, and higher power. Peace within me, peace around me, peace beside, in front of me . . . Peace. As in the serenity of prayer we can and must, in the course of each day, say, "God, Grant me the serenity to accept the things I cannot change; courage to change the things I can, and the wisdom to know the difference."

In all this discussion and sharing of surrender, I have waited until now to discuss one final point. What do we do about suffering, real down to our guts and hearts type of suffering? Those moments of total loss and anguish that enter each of our lives, what of them? What occurs can be illuminated if I may return to the instance I shared with you from my life of being in love and then having to surrender "her," our "relationship." Nothing seemed so painful at the time, so impossible to do. On my knees and with uncontrollable anguish and fears I surrendered, with "not my will, but thine be done." What seemed impossible was now accomplished, "fact," history. The feelings and the reality of our relatinship began subsiding almost at once. Months passed before the feelings of "loss" were no longer a daily occurence. But in their place was a "freedom," a kind of indescribable peace and serenity. No longer was it just a matter of *her* love; rather I came to see Love in the entire world, behind all life, all people. I came to know that love was there for me. Understand this, love will serve your well-being. I learned that the further I entrench myself on my own separate, limited ego and self-will, the greater I truly will suffer, for suffering is separateness from God, from His love, friendship. Suffering comes to us in the form of lessons . . . who we really are and what we really are not. Suffering is our own doing, our own creation as we choose our ego-wills over God's. And there is this distinction that pain is physical and can be inflicted upon us by others, but we inflict pain on ourselves by our own actions or omissions. From the lesson of surrendering my first true love, I learned love was of God, of Self. I learned, too, that with any person I found myself in relationship with, my ego created an attachment to them and their love in such a way that should they leave the scene, our relationship and love would also leave. *That was an illusion.* After surrendering, I discovered that our bonds, our relationship was eternal. That my "yes" of and to love created and assured the existence of that love forever between people who had known each other, of person meeting person, was also seen.

We surrender our suffering, we acknowledge and accept it; unlike our former obsessed states, we do not seek to dull the suffering with pills, drink, food, sex, money, etc. Nothing works when suffering is seen as entirely of our own doing; when the "answer" is surrender to God and His care, the care of His loving relationship in and to us. We walk through our sufferings. Christ was given myrh, a drug to kill pain, by the Wise Men. On the cross, He was offered this drug mixed with wine. He refused. Instead, He did what He had to do and walked through it all; surrendering to His Father, "into your hands I commend my spirit." We are invited to do the same . . . unconditionally. We are offered the same results . . . a joyous rebirth and resurrection in the spiritual Life, with our Friend, God.

ANNE: You know, we think anyone that finds an answer to their personal life is always kind of funny. They are convinced for a while that they are the only ones that have found it, they've discovered it. They are always chagrined to find people who knew that long ago. But I'd like to be able to put into words what we mean when we talk about a spiritual revolution, a spiritual awakening. I'd like to put into words somehow what the "surrender" is and also the fact that alcoholics are people. A lot of them that you talk to think they've discovered some methods, that AA was the first place it was ever discovered. From the beginning of time any spiritual teacher, prophet, writer, or sage all came up with the same answer which is surrender. They called it different things. From Buddah, Mohammed, Christ, Spinoza. They all came up with the same thing right down the line. The ultimate answer is the surrender to a power greater than yourself; the surrender of self-will and in that lies peace, in that lies freedom. That's the thing I feel most strongly about, what I want most to get across to somebody. What do I do about the defects in my character? What do I do about the fact that I self-destroy? What do I do about my neurosis, my compulsion? The answer is surrender and it's the hardest thing to get across to people. That is what I'm talking about when I say it has to be a personal, spiritual experience. Surrender. I once heard a man say in front of about 600 people, a man who had been through tremendous pain, whose life really was a modern day prodigal son, "I would give my very life if I could tell just one person." Then he went on to say, "But I can't. It's such a personal experience."This sounds like such a way out flat statement, but I truly believed it in the end. That is the individual answer for a human being. It's a totally and absolute unconditional surrender to your God as you understand Him.

Twelve
WORKING WITH OUR FEELINGS

Within the Christian tradition and teachings there rests a path, a spiritual way to go which for us becomes our next step. Thus far our maps have read: admit we are helpless in our ego-centered, obsessive life; approach a working belief and relationship with God as we know Him in our personal way; surrendered ourselves, our lives and will over to the gentle care of our God, this Life within us and all living things. Now we begin the task of working with our feelings and going some steps further than what psychology has told us about emotions. We enter into a spiritual process of reconstructing our emotions, altering the very realities that gave rise to those feelings.

About Those Emotions

We must draw near to our feelings, ourselves, our lives and our relationship with others and do all this with total honesty, openness and a willingness to change, to open ourselves up to the healing life force of our caring God. Looking at our emotions we find the following understandings and principles helpful:

> Emotions simply are, and as such, are not to be judged "good" or "bad," but accepted as just *there.*
>
> Emotions are to be acknowledged, accepted; not suppressed, denied, or rationalized away. We cannot say "I am tired" when what we really are is bored, or fearful.
>
> Emotions are to be shared when appropriate.
>
> Emotions are of *our doing. Other people do not create emotions in us. Thinking that they do is a denial of our responsibility for our own emotions. As we have*

created our feelings, so too we can change them, surrender them.

Feelings are to be brought out of the control of our ego and into their proper source, our "self." They are to be subject to our spiritual centers.

Emotions are to be enjoyed when they are positive and learned from when they are negative; that is anger and fear are telling us something about ourselves . . . listen.

Emotions are to be lived in a full experience. If we are feeling something, really feel it.

Emotions are to be surrendered in that no emotion should control us; no feeling should have us addicted to it.

Emotions are what they are and nothing else. Hence, if we are afraid, full of fear and apprehension, we should not suppress that fear and show anger instead.

In light of these principles and the whole question of working with and communicating our feelings Why Am I Afraid to Tell You Who I Am and *The Secret of Staying in Love* by John Powell are recommended. Reading steps 4 through 10 in the *Twelve Steps and Twelve Traditions* of Alcoholics Anonymous would also be helpful.

Now we are ready to go beyond psychology and into a direct application of the spiritual life. We must now make what has been known in Christianity as an examination of conscience. This is a moral house cleaning, a finding out who we really are, what are all those obsessions of ours we were so busy covering up . . . a kind of spiritual Watergate.

Approching ourselves and this examination of conscience after a meditation and prayer is helpful. We will find ourselves more quiet and hopefully less defensive, putting aside our excuse mechanisms we have used to avoid our real selves. We need to also lay aside our pride, our self-righteousness, and just be *honest*. Just pick one sore spot, perhaps your greed. Look at it. Acknowledge you are greedy, you want far more than you need or could ever use. We are greedy because . . . we fear, we are insecure, we want people to look up to us because we have "made" it . . . pride on top of greed. Being *human*, getting down with the rest of humanity is what this process is all about; seeing who and what we really *are,* forgiving ourselves, that enthusiastic willingness to move on and up from here, to release and surrender those weaknesses and unwanted ego involvements of ours. We may find it helpful looking at ourselves in view of the Seven Deadly Sins of pride, greed, lust, anger, gluttony, envy, sloth . . . and how we have practiced them, made them into our obsessions, an art!

This step of consciousness-life examining, our moral inventory, will be different for each of us. Some of us may find the going extremely difficult . . . pride. Others will find it necessary, all of us, to ever so often spend a quiet space of time with ourselves, reexamining ourselves, keeping our self honesty and openness current, updating our willingness to grow.

From this step we move on to a kind of confession. It really does help to unburden ourselves to another human being. But first we need approach our God and show by our openness with Him just how real our trust is. With Him we can tell it all, release and surrender it all.

Doing this we seek out a confidant, a friend we can trust as we share our heart and soul with, the exact nature of our transgressions. We need to do this with another human being, not just with God. In this process, depending on the depth of our former obsessions and the extent of our dishonesty, we will need someone to give us a direct, here and now feedback to what we reveal and share. Our former rationalizations and "insanity" could cloud the purity and thoroughness of our confessions. And we must take this step, practice our moral sharing with another person on a regular basis.

The fruits of these revelations are immediate and powerful. We begin to feel released of all that guilt, fear, pride, etc. we carried around our necks, drawing us into our own ego. No longer do we feel separate from the rest of humanity . . . but a true brother, equal in our humanity to *anyone.* For we have all failed our true self, what we could be, what we are now called to be in the life of the Spirit. Now we begin to see anew; see ourselves as we really are, and other people as they really are . . . and as they, like us, are called to become.

In this sharing of self with another, we begin experiencing a closeness to not only our confidant but other people. The reality of ideas and feelings, held once to be all that there was, now is replaced slowly by the reality of persons, of relationships and sharing. Self replacing ego brings about in us an enthusiastic experience of Life.

Our next step in dealing with our feelings, our moral character defects and ego entanglements, is sensing our readiness to really have God remove all those defects. This is a reapplication of unconditional surrender and humility. We must acknowledge God as the one reality in our lives who really can do something about who we are. For so long we labored in vain to do it all. Now we listen to the inner workings of our heart for that "yes, I am yours God. I am ready to have you heal me, cleanse, forgive, and make me whole again. Your will be done in my life, our life together. Take from me these defects of character which served no one, aided no one, allowed growth to stop and actually retrogress. Fill me instead with You, a knowledge and enthusiastic joy to do your will, which can only be for the perfection of love within me, the completing of the fulness I am called to, the realization of a peaceful happiness and the open sharing of all your new creation with my fellow man." As we move from our obsesssions, defects, moral failings into living from our Self, a Self one with God, the former flow of negative feelings and obsessions ceases. They have no ground to grow in. This, then, is the true mastery over our feelings and our ego.

We are next asked to share our new found spirit by forgiving all harm done to us by others, but especially making things right with all the persons we have harmed. The essence of this is found in Christ's admonition, "do not let the sun go down on your anger."

Those whom we have harmed we must approach with a spirit of humility, undo the harm as we can, and where it is impossible, or unwise, then at least do it in our hearts. This done, and it will be completed over the years and redone whenever we need to, we begin feeling a greater sense of freedom, of truly being one with our fellow man. No longer need we defend, compete, battle, lie, fear; now a sense of oneness along the same path, in the same spirit, takes place with those we meet. Yes, we are all at different places in this garden of God's. Yes, some of us are still lost in our ego, suffering with our obsessions; others are just coming to know the spiritual life. Some are bearing real fruit, for themselves and for others. Yet, we are all one, to be accepted for *who* we are, in spite of *where* we are . . . the Father of us all has called us to this reality.

ANN: She's slipped back, she's super defensive, she's super competitive with the other girls. Everybody is against her. Again, this is the way she was when she first came here. It was pointed out to me yesterday that she had been slipping back for quite a while. The girls were complaining about some of her behavior. She's very hard on her roommate. Just totally nasty. I went to talk to her yesterday. We got to talking and I asked her, what are you doing, what have you been doing? Well, come to find out, she had done two things in the last two weeks: she had stolen something from her employer, from the gal that she works for and she had gone to bed with this guy on a weekend that was really below her standard of behavior. Okay, so to those two things a parent would say, perhaps, that's bad. You shouldn't have done that, have gotten upset about that. Instead of telling her that's bad, you know you are a tramp, you went to bed with this guy, you are a thief, you stole from this woman, I tried to point point out to her and was finally able to make her see, that what she had done was not "bad." What she had done was to hurt herself. She was immediately super defensive. Instead of judging her, I was telling her that these things are things that you cannot do because these things make you feel bad about *you*, you fight everybody around you. You defend yourself on every front, on every level. You are super judgemental about other people and your behavior is rotten. You put yourself in a position where everybody is angry with you. You know those were also two secrets up until we talked about them. Nobody was going to punish you, so you punished yourself. You put yourself in a position where everybody is going to dislike you. You defend something nobody else wants you defending. Just because of these two things. Now whether they are wrong or right is none of my business. What I am concerned about is what are they doing to you? These were both behaviors below your standards for yourself. We watch people paint themselves into a corner. We watch them take the good things in their life and destroy them. We watch them take relationships, and women do this a lot, and destroy that relationship, ruin it, ruin a good job. And we ask ourselves, why is that person so hard on himself? You show me somebody that behaves in that way and I'll show you somebody that's got a secret guilt, that is behaving in a way that is below their own standards of themselves. They don't like themselves and I think that it's very important to know this, especially when dealing with teenagers and young people. I often ask the question, "What did you ever do that made you dislike yourself? You couldn't have done anything that awful. What did you do?" I had a very interesting situation recently. This is not uncommon, one of the things in our society we don't talk much about, yet. There is a tremendous amount of incest in our society today, and more than we have any idea of. I was talking with a young girl the other day who had this secret in her life for a long, long time, the fact that she had sexual relations with her father continuously and over a period of time. She finally got this out. Her father was 35 at the time and she was 12. She felt terribly guilty. I dug and dug and talked and talked and finally the secret was not that she had had the relation with her father, but that she had liked it. That was the secret. When I threw that at her, it was like a slap in the face with cold water. Her face turned as white as a sheet. When I got through to her by simply saying, "How could you have not enjoyed it, it felt good, didn't it? Then why should you have not enjoyed it?" I don't know. It was like a dam broke. This child has been systematically destroying herself since she was twelve years old. Not because she did this with her father, but because she liked it. That was a standard below her behavior. You talk to a religionist, to many, many people, parents, whatever, that's a naughty thing. Here is a twelve year old child whose father touched her in certain areas of the body and it felt good. She feels guilty. She finds out later that it's not the right thing to go to bed with your father through listening to other kids and just growing up and hearing things. Then she realizes she really liked it. Ask yourselves, what would happen if she went to a priest, clergy, minister, mother? What would they have said? Exactly what they said to her. She was evil, she was bad, she was horrible. When I finally was able to tell her, why shouldn't you have enjoyed it, she couldn't answer. She said it felt good. But don't you see that when he wanted to stop, I didn't? Of course you didn't. And finally she said that she didn't know that was wrong and that's the thing you did with boys either. She said, "That's when I found out." It damn near destroyed her. When she finally confessed it to her mother, her mother said it was evil, bad, and all these things."

ANDREA: I'd like to make a comment. The same thing happened to me as a child for four years. I allowed the molesting to go on for four years. There was such a conflict within me and when I finally admitted to it, told my mother because I was really going off the deep end, they wanted to put me in a mental institution. Years later I went to a marriage counselor and when he brought that out; he asked, "Why did you let it go on for so long?" He explained to me exactly what Anne said to me. I didn't hear that part. I went home and attempted suicide. I could not touch my body or look at it any longer because it had finally come up. That was one of the hardest things, one of the biggest secrets in my life when I came to the program and took my inventory. The lady that I took it with luckily said those things that Anne said to that girl. Those sexual experiences are so important and now I'm really grateful that I went through that so that I could share it with that young girl yesterday, because she is a mess. She feels dirty and rotten. My mother never said that I was evil, but she gave me a lot of dirty looks. She rejected me a lot because she lost. She had to divorce her husband. She kicked him out. I felt to blame. It was my fault. I did not want to hurt my mother. I loved her, I didn't want to hurt her and I was constantly her source of irritation. And that was the last straw that broke the camel's back because she loved that man. He left and then she had to go through the pain of taking me to some more psychiatrists and finding out some more things. Up until I really was able to admit that I enjoyed sex; it feels good, I wasn't set free at all. It was horrible and it has only been in the last couple of years and having someone that has a healthy attitude toward sex that my attitude has gotten healthier. I wanted to make that comment because it's not an isolated case. It happens all the time. We just think it's rotten. Why? Because that is what we are told.

PHILIP: What are these little defense mechanisms that teenagers use to get away from feelings, only to hide one feeling with another?

ANNE: The most common is fear. They hide it with anger and hostility, adults too. Anger and fear is manifested not only with hostility but the macho image that some boys develop. "Cool," "super cool," aloof, above it all. All these things develop. I think that fear accompanies an obsessive-compulsive personality, with an addict, an alcoholic. All their feelings are fear.

PHILIP: I remember once dealing with a group of seniors in high school. In the environment of the school, whether they were class officers or worked on the school newspaper, they projected a total sense of self-confidence. They knew who they were; they were adults in every sense. A few weeks after they graduated, I talked to the same group of kids. They were now like scared rabbits, completely turned about. Within the context of their own environment, their fears were covered up because they had been functioning in a familiar school environment.

ANNE: Oftentimes here we see a youngster grow and progress to the point where it's time for him to go out in the world. Kids are together and doing fine and have gained an understanding of themselves and are dealing with their problems. They are safe and functioning well within this environment. They go out to work and two days later they are back again. Terrified. All the old feelings are back. All the old inadequacies, all the old defences are back. Most of them walk through that. Some of them don't. Some of them we have to make them quit working for a while, and get them back here to deal with those feelings thay had at work before having another shot at it. A troubled person, adults included, need a totally safe environment for a period of time. The transition from that safe environment to functioning in the general world is a crucial period. I don't know any way to make it easier except to do it slow. I would prefer, for instance, to have seniors in high school have something similar to a half-way house. Maybe if seniors in high school got a job while they were in high school in the field they are studying, or if they spent part of their senior year at a college several days a week preparing themselves to go from one thing to another, the transition would be smoother. Transitions are very difficult for everybody. For an obsessive-compulsive personality, it's dreadful, it's a crisis.

PHILIP: If you take a look at our culture in the past years of this century, you find we have gone from an immigrant neighborhood environment, where everything was already set, that you never left the neighborhood, that you married a person within a few blocks of you, a relatively safe environment, to the point now where we have become competely migratory. One out of four Americans moves every year. That's a shock to the system in many ways and obviously people in this country are not dealing with it successfully as evidenced by the rise in the use of drugs, tranquilizers, and everything else to anesthetize the person.

ANNE: I have a tendency to oversimplify. I feel there are very few truths. I think the world's been changing for centuries and every generation changes. There are new threats, new problems, new everythings. There is no other generation who has faced total annihilation. The problems may differ but I still think the answer is the same. It's the security, the safety, the sense of being, the sense of home and safety . . . this has to come from within. And certainly all these outside and environmental changes and life style changes have a tendency to shake people up. But the center still has to be the center and if it is not within ourselves, then all the safety in the world isn't going to change it. If we were to suddenly go back to the neighborhood, we would find disturbed people there, too. Progress is progress, and it isn't going to stop. We are going to continue to change. It begins and ends with us. It begins and ends in the center. I found it in myself recently. I'm not sure if our geographical location is going to stay the same, if we are going to have the money, etc., etc. Everything is changing in my life. I can easily rationalize. I can't buy that because of what is going on in my life, I have less time for prayer and meditation. I have spent less time centering myself. Consequently, I have set myself in all kinds of different directions. Here again is that thing of finding your own, a philosophy for your life.

PHILIP: What was your experience in the high school when you were there talking to the kids about feelings?

ANDREA: I did a switch around. I asked them some questions because I was being honest when I asked, "I don't know what it's like to be normal." I have been told that I have a warped mind and I've gone along with what I think worked. So I asked the kids if you have a fight with your boyfriend, what do you do with those feelings? Nobody could answer me. They just looked at me and shrugged their shoulders. If you don't clamp in your system to stop those feelings, what do you do with them? I didn't know what to do with them because I was told, "Well, you act silly, you shouldn't feel that way." Well, what prepared me not to feel that way was when my mother went through all that. I mean totally, ridiculous, immature stupidity. When I was sixteen or seventeen I was competing with my mother for dates, for God's sake! Of course my mother had to date, but she was dating guys young enough to date me. They'd walk out from a date with her and on the sly ask me to go out with them. I don't know how many kids go through that. I know there's not just a few. What do you do with the feelings? I shoved them down. I was told I wasn't supposed to feel that way. You're told to respect your parents; do this, do that. Why? The parents say respect me and turn around and lie to you. Kids are not allowed to sit down and tell a person, "I don't care how old you are, I don't like what you're doing. You don't do that to me, I'm worth more than that."

PHILIP: You are referring to the fact that these teenagers are in a position where a lot of the times they have legitimate anger feelings towards those in authority. Just because a person is in authority doesn't mean they are doing the right thing at all. They have justifiable anger, but society doesn't allow many legitimate expressions for that anger.

ANDREA: No, hell no! What do they do if a kid is really angry and goes up to his teacher and says, "I don't feel this grade is justified. I really worked hard." And for him, he probably did. And the teacher just pooh-pooh's it away. That's too bad. I gave you a grade. I don't know if that is true today; it was true when I was going to school. I worked as hard as I was capable of working. There are a lot of situations where teenagers have emotions which are just not accepted by the adults around them. If a kid stands up in a room and explains, the teacher only hears the scream. He doesn't hear what is underneath the scream, and takes it personal. They take the kid out of class and the kid might be screaming for help . . . there might be a whole bunch of things going on in his personal world and it has nothing to do with school. They don't deal with what's going on. They deal with history, mathematics, sociology.

PHILIP: In other words, everything that is not feeling?

ANDREA: There are no feelings. You don't express your feelings; the feelings are not valid. Maybe a kid had a fight with his mom that day and the kid carries it to school because what does a kid do with the feelings of anger and frustration on the way to school? He might smoke a joint and make it better. Maybe in class he starts coming down on himself and it all comes back.

PHILIP: What do people do in terms of feelings to get them to the point where they really want to use something in order to cover them up?

ANDREA: They push them down because they are unacceptable. My feelings were always unacceptable to other people as a child.

PHILIP: Those feelings, you know how to work with them now, don't you?

ANDREA: Most of the time I do. Sometimes I still don't. Sometimes I have to go up and say I feel like you're really pissed at me, that I've really done something wrong, not with the intent to make them feel bad but with the intent to see me more clearly 'cause I can't see me clearly. I can't turn my head and work on me. It'll kill me.

PHILIP: Mentioning these things in which we use our emotions, some young people certainly use their intelligence and the whole process of being a good student, of being a well-read student, of being an intellectual, a brain or whatever you want to call it, as being a way in which they more or less avoid their emotions. They try to avoid being around their parents and cause conflicts or get involved in athletics where they are allowed to show a lot of frustrations and angers. They just know it, generalize it, they are not too specific where that anger is coming from. But at least it is released in them. Of course you can always involve yourself in some sort of sexual relationship in high school. That allows a lot of expression of pent up feelings. I'm just adding to what you've already said in terms of what so-called normal people do with those emotions and feelings. Very few adolescents know how to handle their feelings by sitting down with themselves and dealing with them. But they do find these other channels that are somewhat legitimate where they can express their feelings. Later on, perhaps in their twenties or thirities, they experience the residue, the effect of those feelings that deep down are still there. Then they enter upon a very confused time in their lives.

In other words, when you look at yourself and you accept your humanness, that's the beginning of some sort of change?

ANDREA: Yeah, I believe so. We laugh and joke in A.A. about rising above all human feelings. We laugh about it, but that's really a serious thing. Recently I came to the conclusion that until I admit and accept my humanness, I can't get to my God as I understand Him. I have to become what He created before I can get to Him. All these years I've spent trying to rise above all those human feelings and not get through to them. I'd go from A to C without going through B, and it doesn't work that way.

PHILIP: In other words, you have to stop running from your very existence, maybe that's the way of needing a rest?

ANDREA: Yeah, I think society looks down on laziness. Work is a virtue. I believe that. I think that if we learn not to listen to our bodies and our innermost selves, which I have a hard time doing because I'm not worth anything, then I won't accept being tired. I won't accept that feeling of wanting to do anything. I don't listen to the message my body is giving to me. I am programmed to be busy. I am what I do. If you don't do well in school, then you don't have a good mind. If you don't mind the rules and do what you are supposed to do, then you're a rotten son-of-a-bitch or juvenile delinquent. If you don't do the meals every night on time, then your husband is going to complain because you're not doing what you're supposed to be doing. Right? I am what I do and that isn't true. I don't know what I am yet, but I have been going under the pretense that I am what I do.

PHILIP: If you were doing a lot of things which you thought people or society expected you to do, and internalized it so you even expected it of yourself, then granted you are doing a lot of things, but they're really not coming from you. In other words, I feel that possibly if you are doing things which are coming from you at a gut level, you would find that a worthwhile expression of your identity.

ANDREA: Yeah, I understand now. When I was growing up I tried to do what my mother wanted me to do. I was incapable of doing that, therefore I was the imperfect child. Now I pretty much do what I want to do. At least that is what I believe; more so than I've ever done before. Now I have another desire and hopefully I will get to do that desire and handle it in the way I see fit. Maybe that is my expression that I will be what I am.

Thirteen

MEDITATION AND PRAYER

In the process of turning away from our old ways, our obsessed egos, we came to a spiritual awakening. We accepted God's active presence in our lives, having surrendered them and our wills to His care. We have fearlessly, honestly, openly searched our souls for moral failings, ego defenses, excesses of self-will and desires. These we have accepted as our own creation, owned up to them, accepted responsibility for them, forgiven ourselves these transgressions. We have humbly shared this total package we found ourselves to be with another human being we could trust, holding back nothing. Humbly we asked God to remove all these shortcomings and moral weaknesses, all our obsessions and ego supports. At the same time we sought out those people we have harmed, righted the wrongs where and when we could; where it proved not wise or not possible we did amends in our heart. Throughout our lives we continue to admit our emotions and failings when they arise, keeping up on our spiritual house cleaning. Throughout all this we turn to our new found friend, our higher power—God. We actively seek to do His will. Now we need to learn and practice on a regular basis, the spiritual habit of talking with and being in close touch, a conscious awareness of God . . . prayer and meditation.

When we begin upon a new and sincere friendship, anyone of us realizes that such a relationship can grow only as we invest ourselves in it. We make time for our friend, times to share, play, love, communicate, learn just who the other is. Doing this, we come closer to discovering who we really are. As our friend accepts us, we feel that "free space" to be ourselves, to unfold feelings, yearnings, concerns, and joy . . . saved only for those we trust most deeply. We find ourselves growing, expanding, pushing out to further reaches of our happiness.

In the spiritual life, we can be no different with God. We, in order to have life and to know it abundantly, must actively pursue our friendship, taking time often to improve our conscious awareness of Him, His will, His presence in our heart.

We in the West live basically a life of distractions. Always and everywhere there is the presence of noise—TV, radio, movies, stereos, etc. We are bombarded with things to *do,* places to go, people to see. Entertainment, sports, and the media combine on their assault on our attentions. Life for many of us is a process of overstimulation and distraction. To prove this, just sit down in a room, a quiet room. Close the door, make sure no one will bother you. No TV or radio is allowed. Just sit. Listen to what is going on inside of you. Do you find yourself deluged in urgings within to get up and *do* something, to break the silence, satisfy some desire? Is there an ever present flow of ideas and/or feelings in your head? Is there ever any real silence, peace? And how long is it before you just can't stand it any longer?

You have just taken your ego temperature to see how entrenched your ego is in your consciousness. What is meditation going to do? If done regularly and honestly, it will serve as a chief means to disattach our consciousness from our ego, put an end to that ceaseless, harassing flow of ideas, feelings, desires. It will help put our self in our center, and our centered self in God. It will give God a chance to "speak" to us, for our friendship to develop.

Remember all those confused states of mind where we were playing child, parent roles; dominating others or being controlled by them? When we were addicted to our emotions or unhealthy relationships, obsessions? When we yearned for peace, a refuge from the chaos and insanity of our ego centered behavior? Well, this meditation practice really socks it to them, gets the job done, releases us from all that garbage we have floating inside.

The Practice of Meditation

We begin our journey inwards to our self through meditation, with the surrender of who we are. We come seeking no certain ends, have no expectations or goals. Like our heart beat, we just let it happen.

Structure

We will meditate in as quiet a place as we can. Try and avoid meditating after eating. The best time is just before eating. Find yourself in a comfortable position, not necessarily lying down, but sitting in a straight position . . . be comfortable, however. All the emotions we have repressed—anger, resentments, fears, hostilities, etc. are still within us. We have locked them away in our muscles, our body . . . that's where all that tension and tightness comes from. As we meditate, we are going to hear from our bodies. To help release some of this tension, do this: tighten up as much as you can all the muscles of your body, including your face. Do so that your body is actually shaking, the strain is so much. Remain like this for twenty seconds or so. Then *slowly* release, starting with your feet and working on up to your face. You will find yourself quite relaxed . . . close your eyes.

Now begin focusing your attention to your breathing. Listen to each breath, each inhalation and exhalation. Never lose the flow; listen, feel . . . "I am," in each breath. Remain quiet.

The ego will *not* like this meditation business. It has weapons to fight back. The body will begin releasing its tensions in the form of emotions, desires will flow in front of you, seeking to take your attention off your breathing. Ideas will assault your mind-consciousness. Fantasies and imaginings will bombard you. OK, we have a response . . . surrender all you see, feel, think. Just let them all "go." It's like watching a movie screen, and you're in the front row . . . do not allow yourself to become a part of the movie! You see, the ego doesn't want to relinquish its cherished position of number one. We must allow awareness to enter our self, however. During our meditation, this going deeper into our self will realize a change in the color patterns we see before our eyes; some people claim a slight sensation of "falling" into the self, in a gentle sort of way. All this time we continue to turn our awareness to our breathing. At some point we will no longer be aware that we are breathing; will actually lose contact and feeling with the rise and fall of our chest and diaphram . . . good; we're getting there, approaching the self.

Follow this technique for twenty minutes to a half hour, once in the early morning, and later afternoon. To really develop this spiritual tool, we must be faithful in our practice, consistent. We may set aside longer blocks of time. There is no time schedule. Our meditation will go differently for each of us.

As we do our meditations, following the flow of our breathing, surrendering, disattaching ourselves at whatever ideas, images, desires, feelings arise, we will begin to approach our center, our self. As we do, there will be no sense of time, even noise will be reduced considerably. There will be a sense of peace, of completeness, of well-being. At our centers, in our self, we can rest, hangout, let things be, let us just "be." In this place, there are no judgments, no distractions, no urgings, no ego, ideas, feelings. All is restful, bliss. After a meditation at this level, and having rested in our "self," we will find as we return to our daily business of living that we cease taking things personal, that our ego begins to listen to the direction of our centered self. People are no longer a threat, or we release our feelings of control, dependencies, chaotic, undirected energy. We learn to focus our energy on the tasks before us, the will of God in our lives. We do not give people power over us, responding helplessly to everything they do or say. We walk a spiritual path, coming from our self within. Yes, there is the benefit of being relaxed, but so much remains in our meditation.

The Work of Meditation

Finding ourselves at our center during meditation is not meant to be an end in itself. Christ gave us the example that just before He began His Father's work, He spent 40 days in the wilderness in prayer and meditation. When we discover ourselves in our Self, at our center, we find a totally accepting place—no judgments allowed; we are on safe grounds. In this place we can accomplish the work of our examination of conscience, taking our self inventory—observing, accepting, and forgiving ourselves *without judgment.* Clearly we can see the true state of our relationships with people, who and how we have harmed anyone. Here we can gather ourselves together to present to our confessor, friend and confidant, what we have chosen to see as our humanity. In this place of peace we more sincerely approach our God as we ask Him to humbly remove our defects of character and reveal His will in our life to us.

We may also choose to meditate with someone else, someone we seek closer ties with . . . after meditation our sharings of self flow with a joyous ease. Or perhaps we need confront someone with our feelings, concerns, a truth. Then do so after meditation. Meditation releases energy within us, makes it avaliable to do God's will in our life. We are refreshed at the very source of Life itself. Nothing we've ever known has been able to do this for us. Yet we must be patient in our meditations to experience their fruits, seeking God's caring help in opening us up to our selves.

We Meet Our God . . . In Prayer.

Meditation is a way, an activity. Yes, we meet our self, our peaceful centers. Beyond our self is the universal Self, in whom we have our being, our joy. While we are in our center, we are in a position to develop our conscious contact with God, expand our friendship. I address God as "You," as "I am who I am," and as "Father." At peace within myself, I stand in relation to *the* person in my life. I talk with my Friend, reveal all that I know myself to be. This is prayer. Here I am not held back, and can freely thank God for life, acknowledge His as my Life, expres my love for Him, my joy in His free and unconditional love for me. I sense the full meaning behind the word life, the love behind and in it. Here I seek to know His will for me in my life and the strength to carry it out. As I meet and talk with God, I continue to discover His presence in the world, in all of His creation. His being known as "I am who I am" allows me to feel at home everywhere, His Presence and support behind every difficulty and concern. Identify with the writers of the Psalms, men who looked upon the face of God in their hearts and who know the joyous truth of His relationship to others. Our hearts *are* restless until they rest in Him, our God.

"Why does meditation work?" Look at it this way. List all of the things you enjoy and all the most meaningful, joyful, happy moments of your life. Now, when did these moments take place—in the past, future, or present? In the present, clearly so! Everything we taste, touch, feel, smell, hear is *always* here and now. Life takes place in the present. Our egos put us into a guilt-past, fear-future orientation. Yet in the present is joy, living! That's why sex is such a concern . . . it *really* draws us into *now.* And God named Himself as "I am who I am," not "I was," or "I will be." God is in the present, too. To live in the present is at least living within the same time frame as God. It remains up to us to turn our self to the person of God. In meditation we focus on the most immediate and present experience available to our consciousness . . . our breathing. Who ever *missed* a breath because they were living out some past or future involvement!?

So the more focused and honest we are in tuning into our breathing, the sooner we begin discovering the here-and-now self of who is *doing* the breathing. In moving away from the *future,* we leave behind anxiety, fear, and insecurity—the emotions of a future-oriented ego. In withdrawing and closing up shop on our *past,* we leave behind pride and guilt. In the present . . .peace, joy, love.

There is another form of meditation, active meditation. In this we practice nonjudgment. Simply spend several hours walking, looking, observing people, places, things without judging, or forming opinions about them. Let your five senses and not your mind do the experiencing. Allow things just to "be," asking nothing from anyone, or anything; let things alone; this is the practice in letting the world "unfold" to us. Do this meditation several hours each week and see what "happens."

Fourteen

PLAYING, CREATING — REDISCOVERING THE CHILD WITHIN

Throughout my childhood, into adolescence, one of my most painful frustrations was my inability to play and enjoy myself. As a child I grew up in neighborhoods where roving bands of teenage gangs threatened the very survival of anyone younger than they. As a teenager I separated myself from many people out of my fear on the one hand and a glaring sense of superiority on the other. Having "fun" was more work than pleasure. Things began changing during my late teens and early twenties, and I attributed it to the results of following a spiritual path. Now, as an adult, I find that too many people I meet find it hard to let go and enjoy each day as it happens. I sometimes feel like a kid let out to play after the rain, only to find that everyone else's mother has kept them inside!

With the more intense obsessions of alcoholism and drug addiction, the common denominator is the same . . . no one knows how to enjoy themselves, to let the little kid in them out to play. But being clean and sober alone isn't going to take care of the problems of boredom, of living with a sense of zest and vitality. This next spiritual development in our growth calls for us following Christ's admonition, "Unless you become as little children, you will not enter into the Kingdom of God."

If a person follows the spiritual program thus far discussed, that little child starts peeking his head out, getting a little more bold and flexible, and begins to explore the world anew.

The Japanese have this saying, "The first duty in life is to enjoy it." Following the spiritual steps we begin seeing that no one else can have our fun for us; that we can't be dependent on other people to show us a good time, to entertain us. Indeed, we must take to heart this duty of enjoying life, and make a personal commitment to do just that! We can *choose* to have a good time if we want it. Try starting a day where you focus on and repeatedly reaffirm to yourself that "today" I will enjoy myself, and do it! Make it a point to *treat yourself* today. There is a lady in her 80's who was interviewed and asked the question, "If you had to do it all over again, what would you do differently?" She replied, "I'd take off my shoes earlier in the spring and go barefoot a lot longer into the fall, and I'd eat plenty more ice cream!" That's the spirit; we must explore ourselves and find out just what we can do to have fun.

If there are doubts in our minds as to enjoying life's business, where might our problems arise? How are we going to get where we want to go?

Modeling

If we were raised in situations where we rarely played with anyone else, then *now,* at whatever age we are, we need to *learn* from someone how to play. Go down to a park sometime and observe kids at play, or babysit sometime and let those 4, 5, 6 year olds get you "involved." One can also look around and examine those people you know as to who *really* knows how to have a good time, and who doesn't. Hang around those who *do*!

Confronting Our Negative Parent

Plenty of people share their feelings that when they are about to enjoy themselves, a voice comes over them saying, "You don't *deserve* to have a good time," "What have you done to *earn* this fun," "You're not acting 'grown up,'" etc. Just aim both barrels at that negative parent and put those voices to rest. Meditation does much towards freeing us of those tape recordings, those voices which keep us from enjoying ourselves. We must realize we are loved by God totally, we must love ourselves totally, and from this love will spring our inspiration to enjoy the life we have been given. Allow our adult to intervene and talk to that "parent," pointing out that yes, we *will* have a good time, it being for our own welfare.

Learning New Games, Flexibility

You don't have to be "good" at something to enjoy it! So many of us shy away from learning new fun things like ice skating, bowling, tennis, because we are worried about *performance.* Let's put that concern to *rest.* Just get into whatever you are doing; the enjoyment follows. Trust, trust surrender.

Expanding Our Horizons, What's Over the Hill

Take the whole world as *your* personal "playground." Feel comfortable at *home* in your newly expanded world. People *don't* bite. Visit those places you always wanted to visit, not just foreign countries, or surrounding states. Sure, take on the world; but remember, too, that the world is our own state, the mountains, beach, or desert nearby . . . your own valley and city . . . your own neighborhood.

Run in the Sun; Sports

Take on a new sport or two, or replay those sports that you once loved. Join a bowling league, a tennis center and ladder; a ski group. Get on a city and park recreation basketball, volleyball, softball team. Run, jog; go to the beach and run, to the mountains to hike and climb. Get a frisbee and throw to your heart's content. What have you got to lose? A *good* time if you don't!

Music

Expand what musical tastes you have. Ask your friends to play for you their three or four *favorite* albums . . . you're sure to hear something new to enjoy. *Sing* . . . make a list of songs you really like and buy a songbook with them in it. Then learn the words and whenever you feel that free spirit within or whenever you *want* to feel that free spirit . . . sing. Go see the "Sound of Music" and learn from Maria's sense of joy.

Become Friends with Nature and Nature's God

Set aside time to quietly, deliberately be in natural settings, with friends but also *alone.* Alone with the quiet, still beauty we do feel God's presence and our own inner peace and strength. How often do we treat ourselves to this blessing?

Vacations, "Free Days," an "Adventure"

So many of us do not take that needed vacation; instead we work ourselves to a frazzle, or spend hours making up excuses why we aren't taking a vacation. Take a mini-vacation, a day or two somewhere new or old. Give yourself a "free day," a holiday where you wake up, feel good, and take off to some wonderous adventure.

Eat, Drink and Be Merry

Have a pot luck dinner with your friends; go out to that restaurant you've been meaning to visit, cook that special dinner for that favorite someone! Cook . . . learn how to; it *is* fun and creative. Call up your friends on the spur of the moment and invite them over to make pizza or go out to your favorite spot and live it up . . . why do we confine ourselves to Friday or the weekends! Share, share, share!

Massage, Saunas, Jacuzzies

Serve your special treat, a massage, and sauna, and jacuzzi. Have a friend *give* you that massage and give one to them in return. I've taken to heart a favorite biblical story where Jesus visits two single women, Martha and Mary. Martha always runs off to fix Christ a special dinner, while mary annoints and washes his feet with oil and perfume (massage). Christ one day goes up to Martha and informs her that by that close, personal, touching and intimate (affectionate too!) attention, Mary has chosen the better way! Like the bumper sticker says, "Have you hugged your kids today?" Let's not be afraid, but develop to the extent we can, a joyous enthusiasm in embracing our friends, stroking and touching them. One woman I know confided in me she rarely told her children bedtime stories, but never failed to give them a foot or back and neck massage; the relationship of love between her teenage daughters is enviable!

Times Alone

We do not afford ourselves the peace and quiet joy of being alone. By following the spiritual path we are closer to being truly present to our real selves when we are alone. Choose a set time and place ever so often for this self enjoyment. Light several candles in a room, play quiet, mellow music, and just get in touch with yourself. Some of us do this in our bathtubs, or in the back yard soaking up the sun. But we really do need those spaces to ourselves where the stillness and joy of our person can gently surface . . . a serene wood, a walk at sunrise or sunset.

Treat Yourself to Your Friends, Treat Your Friends

How beautiful is a true friend, one of life's greatest treasures. Treat yourself to those friends, special times alone. Most of all, if married, and hopefully to a *friend,* set aside those times together where you can mutually enjoy one another. It is grand to massage one's friends, cook little or big treats for them, bring over favorite albums and books to share.

Have a "Favorite" Party

Invite your friends to share an evening where everyone does those *favorite* things together, teaching and sharing. On the invitations and for suggestions from your guests, have everyone bring their two favorite records, books, poems, a favorite dish, something they like to do to share with the group.

Pamper Yourself

Just treat yourself to that warm bubble bath, listening to your favorite record, burning a scented candle, eating and drinking what you like best, reading a favorite book. Get several people together and have everyone pamper each other.

People, Places, Things

Go see a variety of different entertainers, types of entertainment. In all things remember, try anything once . . . then you can make an honest, nonlimiting judgment. Go to places like art galleries, museums, natural history collections, a new park, the circus, etc. Be in love with the world and all things in it, and you'll be close to living your new found freedom.

The list is endless for enjoying ourselves, but here goes some suggestions to try or just do again.

Treat yourself to: *Expressing yourself through writing, art, music, dance, etc.; caring for a pet, growing a garden, learning new interests, hobbies, fruit and berry picking, a bicycle ride, flowers in the house, your bedroom, playing with children, story telling, spend a day with a friend, spend time doing nothing but observing and looking.*

A massage, go on picnics in the country, get up for a sunrise, observe a sunset, spend time with a full moon, smell the flowers, touch the leaves of trees, look gently and with love into the face and eyes of your dearest friends, be aware of the seasons, their changing moods, textures, colors, smells . . . ice cream, in every form, daydreaming an afternoon away, a hike along some rural path, dancing, running barefoot in the grass, a water balloon fight on a hot day, a weekend in the mountains or woods, a horseback ride at sunrise, full moon; learning one of the arts; painting, ceramics, etc.; go to plays, musicals, raise some house plants, babysit some playful children, etc., etc.

Fantasy Projections, the "Real You"

After a meditation or whenever you're especially centered, ask yourself, "If I could go anywhere, do anything I really always wanted to do, and be and have nothing stop me, what would I do?" Then list all your responses, and for the rest of *your life* commit yourself to doing everything you really wanted to do. Throw off the shackles of fear, lack of self-confidence, and obsessions. As you accomplish each one, you'll discover that the "real you" is a worthwhile enjoyment, that the spiritual path we have chosen is one of true *living,* true joy and celebration.

Fifteen

WORKING WITH OUR FRIEND, GOD . . . SERVICE

As we live our spiritual path we find ourselves going inwards, to our self, to the God-self within. Over time, in and through prayer and meditation, we realize a place of reality, intensely personal, spiritual. Yes, there *is* an inner bliss, we do approach the love that we *are,* whereas once we thought we *had* or *they* had it to give to us. Respond to that love, draw near to the love we are. Surrender all those false ideas we have attached ourselves to: "I am worthless," "I am alone," "I am incapable," "I am insecure." The heart of our being, as we unfold it, shows us a different truth: "I am," "I am peace," "I am joy." We are, in a sense, a frightened child, in our ego, self-will obsessions. Our questions are, "Where are you, my real self?" "Where are you, God?" The answer is "within you, all around you, of and through, behind and before you . . . always and forever. *This* is the nature of things."

To our first concern of what am I to do in this life, we discover that we are to love, to serve the God-love within, manifest this to all we meet in our everyday lives. It becomes a matter of "being" who we really are, our self, our love; this physical universe and our particular culture determines often the *form* of that expression. Some will raise a family, make the world laugh, grow its food, transport us, dress us, write for us, manufacture the conveniences we use, etc. Above this "form," however, is the daily business of relating to people, of developing an attitude of love and service on a one-to-one basis.

At the heart of this service is unconditional love, supported by a set of principles which are no more than ways of seeing and responding to ourselves and others. We put on a new person, a born again person, a spiritually awakened self, and see that same "person" and God's presence in our fellow man.

We Are Working With Our Friend, God

God is love, personal, all in all. Yet our world in its own self-obsessed way, fails to respond to God within. We are judged and reduced to an "idea" . . . Black, Jew, Irish, attractive, status, who we know, who our parents are, how much money we have. We seek personal recognition, of us seeing and relating to the person within the people we meet and having that same response given us. We grow weary of relating only as a *part* of ourselves, a portion of ourselves judged good or bad, stupid or intelligent, ugly or attractive, weak or powerful, known or unknown. When we surrender to ourselves and God within, all this changes in time. We cooperate, if we *choose* to do so, in unveiling the Person and love in us, each other, the "World." In working with God, we are seeking to "Be" our real self, and in so doing, witnessing to His real Self, His total Presence . . ."God, you really are! I really am! You, all the other *selves* and persons in the world, you really are!"

Saying "Yes" to Ourselves, Free and Spontaneous . . . Risk and Trust

Each of us is called to be our own "person," to live *our* own life, not somebody else's. It is our story that needs to be told, owned, created, enjoyed! It is you, and I, that needs to be free. Freedom is no more than loving: ourselves, others, God, the universe in all its manifestations and celebrations (love, friendship, the seasons, rain, sunshine, animals, ice cream!). We are called in the spiritual path to take our life, its happenings and fulfillment, out of other people's hands and power, and give it back to *us,* to our self, to the God within seeking to be in and of our very being, to the awesome love energy within. The whole world *is* ours. In this sense we must trust our feelings and intuitions, respond to them, hold back from judging them or limiting them out of fear. It's a kind of "laugh when something's funny, cry when something is sad," hug, embrace and kiss when you feel it within, don't hold back. Has our inner self inspired us to boldly strike out on our own, change jobs, living environments, life styles . . . then do so if it's really you. Yes, we do risk something, usually an unproductive and unhappy "old self"; trust those inner directives and turn to God within for counsel and confirmation of His will. Our lives *really are* His. And if any questions remain as to our life decisons and directions, the final standard must be, "Is it done out of love?"

Seeing and Accepting

To serve we must "see" what really is going on in ourselves, another person, a given interaction between people. Not our own ego fears, projections, self-will, expectations, and judgments but just what "is." And after seeing what is, *accepting* as real, as the "truth" that which really is. People *do* need confirmation that "they are," and in "all that they are."

Response-i-bility

Seeing and accepting what is, we are called to respond to ourselves and others. Our ability to respond (respons-i-bility) is a direct measure of quality of the love we have for ourselves, God, others. Do we see an unmet need in someone that we can respond to *without* taking away the responsibility they have to *themselves* . . . then we do it. And how this last truth is so important, that we do not serve anyone by making them dependent upon us, or we on them, when they can be doing for themselves. All dependency does is postpone the day when another person (or ourselves) will have to live their own life, attain their own happiness.

On the feeling level, responsibility is weeping with those who weep, laughing with those who laugh. It is sharing in another person's feelings and allowing them to share in our feelings by *expressing* those feelings, freely, spontaneously. As we lower our ego barriers and defenses through living the spiritual life, we more closely approach other people and thus are able to respond to "who" we are now more aware of.

Creating Spaces of Unconditional Love, Support

Our lives are a constant pattern of changes, problems, crisis, and challenges. We are adjusting, always. Deaths, divorces, jobs, changes, friends, relationships, passages in and through adulthood. In the spiritual sense, "we" never change. Our self, our person is the same; complete, self-sustaining. Our ego involvement and interaction with life makes us appear to change as our experiences, knowledge, bodies alter, expand and has us react to life in different ways at different times along the way. Haven't we all known true friends whose inner self we met and no matter how many years pass or what changes they or we go through, we sense "sameness" in our *selves.* When we meet them again, after a long time absent, we just take up where we left off. A real comfort, this person-to-person consistency.

But the vast majority of our relationships sustain upheavals and differences we often feel uncomfortable with. In the spiritual life of service we respond to our fellow man, and to ourselves, by allowing all this change business to take place and refraining from judging the person behind all those changes. Rather, we trust their inner selves to come through, to work out into their consciousness and center. We let them "be," and go through what they have to go through. A secret to this has to do with honesty. Most of us want something from other people and stay in relationships as long as we are getting some "thing." When other people change, often they no longer give us these "things" . . . their good looks, happy times, someone to play with, our sense of importance being with them, etc. Our spiritually renewed self will still continue to accept *them,* and refrain from making demands on them, wanting and expecting things for ourself, using them. We can honestly admit to these real wants and motives, surrender them, and be a support for the growth process taking place in these people we relate to. We serve people by allowing them to "grow," in their own time, in their own way. Parents find this at times painfully frustrating and difficult. They want their children all grown up and "now," they want for them things and a life the parent should really own up to as their self-will projections. Being a parent requires the maturing and practice of patience, accepting one's offspring where they are at, allowing them to live their own life, and giving them unconditional love and support to do this. That support is spelled "encouragement." And these virtues spill over into any and all relationships . . . especially the one we have with ourselves and *our* growth and change.

Accepting From Others

Many of us find it difficult to accept from other people what they are giving, who of themselves they are giving. We need not judge the gift other than "is it personal, aiding my growth, insuring my well being?" Accept all that is good. Be happy in the freedom and love of the giver and enjoy the gift . . . and go, do likewise, give. Accepting allows the full expression of another person's being. Imagine giving love or offering friendship and no one accepting!

Patience

To serve, we come to recognize that there is no time. Our real selves are beyond time and its workings. We simply "are" . . . now. Things do come to pass, there is a time and season for everything. Trust in that. Your most cherished heart desires are working themselves out, like a child coming to birth. Often painful, yet life awaits for those who wait, who trust in the care of God unfolding our lives to us, the proper order of living to us, Himself through and in us. Do not the seasons see the coming to blossom and fruit all manner of life's manifestations? We are one with life. Surrender, accept, respond, love . . . all is complete.

Confronting

Service means saying "no" and "yes" for the well being of each other. Confront with the truth, in a nonaccusing, judgmental way, ourselves *first,* our brothers next. Stand up, express who you are and what you feel, what you're really trying to say, do. What your fears are, when someone has crossed the line on us, when we are afraid, uneasy, let the people who need to know, know. Stop people; when people are needing to feel a real caring from someone they often do outrageous things. They want someone to stop them. Do so, and if it is done out of love and concern, then often the other person will stop themselves.

Unconditional Love

What is this most powerful force in our service to persons? How do we do it? We do it, like all the other spiritual virtues: by simply *doing* it. We refrain from motives, desires, ego-will, judgments:

I'll love you if . . .
I'll love you when you give me . . .
I'll love you when you become . . .
I'll love you just for now . . .
I'll love you as long as . . .
I'll love you when you do . . .

We love:

from our heart centers
freely . . . not counting the cost
in order that we too may live
the person and all that they are
to let God out in you, in them
to let us out of ourselves
to enjoy and celebrate our lives, Life
to enjoy each other
to know self, person
to be free
to be truly ourselves
seeing the coming to be of the other person
to live
because we are . . . of God.

Sharing, Fellowship

People, relationships, sharing is the name of the game. Our spiritual lives are lived with and in people, each other. No longer are we separate from our fellow man, above or below him, superior or inferior. We are one, co-workers in realizing our life, becoming and living and sharing of ourselves.

Special Friends, Soul Mates

Along the way we are going to feel a special kinship to certain of our fellow human beings. It will be a special sense of "living," of being ourselves with them, of feeling especially comfortable around them. There is but one service to these spirits we meet . . . reach out and share that which really "is" between us; take and make those special cherished times of sharing; thank our self for such a gift.

Being All We Can Be

Each of us is called to service by fulfilling the vast potential for loving, living, and laughing each of us has. Expanding the circle of friends, interests, travels, enjoyments, skills, relationships . . . enjoying all of life, being open to it all. Others find it easier and supportive to "be," if we "are," if we are expressing in our lives who we really are and thereby not being so taken up with and bothered by what's going on around us, and what's going to happen next.

Consulting

Ever so often, and for most of us this means plenty, we seek our inner self, the inspiration and promptings, direction of God. He is, after all, our senior partner. This is His life we are born into. So many of our problems and concerns we take on ourselves, really feeling the terrible weight they often mean. Sit down and talk a spell with the one person who does know what's going on, where it's going, and what it all means. And take to heart, also, the counsel of our dear and trusted friends. God works through them. Be open, listen . . . act.

Agreement, Commitments

We are ever making agreements with people to do this, go here, be there, help with this or that. Marriages, jobs, the daily business of living is really the following through on our agreements and commitments. There is nothing more bothersome than to have someone break an agreement . . . it's our quick temperature gauge to finding out if a person is living their lives more from their person or from their ego, and consequently how far we can trust him if he can't trust himself. To serve is to be in agreement, harmony, and to follow through on our agreements and commitments. it also means knowing our limits, just what we can commit ourselves to and to what degree. Growth in the spiritual life allows us at some point to be *total,* totally committed, in total agreement.

Modeling

All of us have found people along the way to admire, who they are, what they have made of themselves. Often, without them knowing it, we have imitated them, patterning some of our life after theirs. Service to others includes being who we are, developing our spiritual characters so that those who are not there yet will have some idea what it is all about, what the results look like. And what's so comforting about this process is that unlike what people say, what a person is, is "real," can be counted on.

Being Who We Are, In Our Service

Perhaps in our concern about the form our service will take, we will come to this reality: that the form, be it a truck driver, a doctor, a baker or whatever, will be in a constant state of change. Even professional people find themselves, i.e., a doctor, going beyond just doing the medical art expected of him and giving counsel, advice, open to people's inner hearts and concerns. The form of the job, the "service" is not nearly as important as being who we are, *as we are doing whatever we are doing.* Being just who we are *is* service.

ANNE: The steps applied to your life must be done on an individual basis. And no one tells you how you should be or how you should act or what you should become. Become whatever you intended to be with the help of these twelve steps. It's a personal thing and that's one of the reasons why I love it. That's one of the reasons why I was able to accept the program. The steps were mine; they were a way of life, my personal way of life becomes whatever I was going to become. There are also people who just don't seem to be. And they are as foreign to me as somebody from a different country. But occasionally I meet someone whom I try to figure out. That's what I do for a living. I figure people out. I turn on my perceptors and I try to figure out what their strengths are, what their weaknesses are, what they're afraid of, where they are coming from. I met a woman recently who, to me, is what I would call normal, well-balanced, a happy human being. When I met her and talked to her and got to know her I asked her some questions without being pointed about how she got that way. She's a woman who came into town, a brand new person, and didn't know anyone. She's an attractive woman with a pleasing personality, so it was easy for her to meet people. But I've never seen, from the time she was brand new in this group that I have, one bit of shyness, discomfort, unsureness or anything. She just came there totally convinced, and I don't think the question ever came up, that she was acceptable. She belongs there, she belongs where she is. She's comfortable within herself and I talked to her trying to find out why. This woman was raised with no organized religion by a mother and father who had a deep belief in God and a tremendous amount of love and warmth. None of that, "You've got to do this, you've got to do that." Her family never attended church and she was never made to attend church. But they had a deep belief in God and talked about it a lot. She was raised with it. I was envious of her, I couldn't help but be. She's young and she is a grandmother. I'm sure as old as I am she looks ten years younger than I do. She's just totally at home with herself and the world. Now this woman is not an obsessive-compulsive personality. She's one of the rare ones I've met, but occasionally I do meet people like that. I always question them about where they came from, where they were born, and get them talking about themselves. I pick that up everytime. From the beginning of their lives rarely do they have a dogmatic religious background. I always ask, "What was your mother like?" They reply something like, "My mother loved me very much. She loved us kids. She taught us all about God. Never was she judgemental, critical." There are people who are not obsessive-compulsive people. That is rare in our society. But you do find it.

PHILIP: I'm also reminded sometimes that people we meet as adults went through something as a teenager. They had some initiating experience with love and it did turn them around tremendously. When I first came to the experience of love for another human being, and then to a spiritual awakening experience at seventeen, I was aware that my life was going to be different from that day on. People who later on met me, classmates of mine from high school, said "Boy, you've changed a lot. You're not as shy. You are totally self-confident about most situations." They never asked why. But had they asked me why, I would have given that experience as the answer. I also think it's a shame, as you said, that our society cannot recognize the total, final, and ultimate importance of raising children and providing them with that nonjudgmental and spiritual foundation. It's just so obvious that this is where the ills of society are not only perpetrated but the positive, the good, can be given to somebody and they can develop themselves from that point. It's unfortunate that the family, the child rearing way of life is not given as much attention as has been true in the past and as it really should be.

ANNE: There is something that has to come first and then we are back at that other thing that I'm fanatic on. What a person often must be given first which enables him to go ahead and get the rest for themselves, find their own answer, is unconditional love. The single thing that happens between a youngster and us here at Turn-Off when they come, and it's like watching a miracle in front row center, is unconditional love. Whatever type of youngster that comes into this house, I don't care if they are one of these acting out types or whether they are totally withdrawn or a sociopath, like one that we have here, whatever the cover is, whatever the method is, whatever type of youngster that we find from the very most difficult ones to reach to the most open ones, that constant unconditional acceptance and love is ultimate. Not because he is good or bad, not because he is an addict or nonaddict, not because he performs well and does his chores well, not because he works the program or doesn't work the program, just an unconditional and constant acceptance and love. I found that in another area, and it thrilled me to death. I was at that Age Hospital Institutional Convention last weekend. There were some inmates, ex-inmates of prison, and they were asked from the audience what it was about Alcoholics Anonymous that was different from other self-help groups that had come into the institutions throughout the time that they were there. Each one went to A.A. meetings within the institutions for different reasons. Some of them went there to see the women, smell the perfume. Some of them went to get out of some duty. Some of them went there searching for something. All different reasons. The reason that the Alcoholics Anonymous got to them when the other programs did not is that over a period of time the same people were there. They never let them down. They continually acted the same, said the same thing. One man said that he went to Alcoholics Anonymous for four years and one man came to the institution every week once a week and and never missed a night. He said, "I'd wait to see if that son-of-a-bitch was gonna show up again. He was just delightful. I knew he was going to lose interest because I never let him know that I gave a damn about what he was saying and that I cared about him at all. I just sat back and said to myself, I'm just going to see how long it's going to take him to where he says, 'screw them, they don't care' and quit coming." Four solid years that man came and he never missed a night. It's a constant and continuous love, reassurance, and reinforcement, all the time, of the person, not of their behavior, not of their performance, but of the person. This guy said, "It was this guy that I didn't like, had nothing in common with, and every Monday night there he was. Week after week after week. Every Monday night I treated him like I couldn't stand the sight of him. I made fun of him, I laughed at him, I argued with him and all he did was smile and say, 'I love you.' Every Monday night."

PHILIP: Let's go on and hear about some of your school experiences.

ANNE: I remember, Phil, I was a typical mess-up in high school and junior high. I went to school all those years and only two teachers knew I was a constant failure, a screw-up, and a trouble maker. One was a man and the other a woman. The man had taught in a home for incorrigible boys and later came to the high school where I attended. I was kicked out of class. My behavior was not bad enough to expel me, but they had to do something with me. . . so, they put me in his class. He was a woodshop teacher in charge of the projection crew. He put the movies on for different classes. He knew exactly what I was. He always told me if I was going to smoke to smoke in a certain room because he knew I was going to do it anyway. He knew I was a very troubled girl. He dealt with me and it was the damndest thing because I knew he was handling me. I was too sharp not to know. Yet, that man did a lot for me in the area of self-worth . . . he knew from my school records, which he looked up, that I was both a bright and troubled person. He taught me how to run a camera and load it. He put me on the projection crew. I was the only girl ever to be on that projection crew. I was his secretary and I took attendance and did all those things. He called me a secretary. He gave me a sense of my own beginning. When I left high school, got married and had a baby, he was the only person that I wanted to show that baby to, the only person. I had given him nothing but trouble all the time. When I had my little baby, brought him home, I wanted to take that baby to school to show to Mr. Howard. And I did. By that time I was an adult, too.

The other teacher was a woman. She was a history teacher and she knew all about me. She never tried to teach me, never gave me an assignment. She had me take roll, run errands for her, do personal typing, and things like that. She loved me; no matter how bad I acted, she just smiled. She never expelled me.

Two teachers in all that time. I think of that when I deal with these kids. So often when I'm dealing with one of these kids, who's a real screw-up, he's really angry, I see myself and I see Mr. Howard. I see it so often because he gave me a sense of my own value. He never emphasized the fact that I was a screw-up as far as school work was concerned. He always emphasized that I was good at running the projector and one hell of a secretary. He never mentioned anything else. What that has to do with him I don't know except that I felt love from him and he never said he loved me, nor did he ever really say he cared about me. Neither did that other teacher, but I knew both of them cared about me. They didn't change, no matter how badly I acted. Consequently, I quit acting bad. It has worked here and there are so many things that I've hit on when working with kids. I think I've hit on most of them because of my own experience and pain. For instance, selfishness. That's one that adults love to say. We deal a lot with selfishness here because obsessive-compulsive people are the most selfish people in the world.

It's that giving you know. It's like you ask me to talk about where I am, how I got to where I am. You see, I think that when I was talking earlier and saying that people don't really want to hear how I got there, they suspect something else, want something else. They want some kind of realistic, dramatic, awakening type of thing. I believe that what I do and what I have learned is a very selfish thing. After all, what are we all concerned with anyway? Whatever we perceive it to be; our own salvation! That's what we are really primarily concerned with. I don't feel good, I don't like what's going on in my life, what am I going to do about it? What I found is strictly a pragmatic thing. I found myself to be one of the most self-centered people that I had come across. I was pathologically self-centered. It was killing me. I couldn't stand it anymore and I couldn't find any way out of it. All I can say is that I felt totally imprisoned by myself, by my wants, needs, desires, hungers and totally self-centered. I was totally out of touch with people. I never touched anyone. I never allowed anyone to touch me beyond the surface . . . and I was just fed up with it. I was brought into the presence of a person that taught me, that loved me totally, unconditionally and completely. Not in spite of what I was, because at that time I was a drug addict, a prositute. . . I was not a nice person, I was totally unlovable. I was hostile and nasty and had used my intellect as a weapon against other people. Through all these things, this person loved me back to life and out of my self-centeredness. I asked many times what is she after. What does she want? What axe does she have to grind? I had nothing she needed. When I left her house and went out on my own again, I asked her what I could do to repay her for what she had given me. She literally healed my self-inflicted wounds and brought me out of that prison. I had no understanding of why it happened or how it happened or what happened. When I asked her what I could do to repay her, she said that she had forged a link in that chain of love and that I was to forge another link in it by giving it to someone else and one day it would surround the world which, sounds very dramatic. I didn't understand what she meant and I didn't know how to do it. The only pattern that I had to go by was the one she taught me. It was the only pattern I had. So I went out and got my own place and began to live my own life, to get a job, etc., and tried to remember what she had taught me. I began to do it. As I did it, the more I invested myself and my love in other people, the less of myself there was. Yet, I was more totally myself. Today, the reason that I do what I do has nothing to do with altruism or anything else. It has to do with the fact that the only way I can stay out of that prison of self-obsession, self-centeredness, is by continuoulsy investing myself in other people . . . continuously giving, loving unconditionally, returning what I was given to another human being. I do not do it because I particularly like to do it. I enjoy the results of it because to me watching someone come alive, who's been walking around dead for a couple of years, is the biggest kick in the world. I do it on a daily basis because to me it has to do with the quieting of the ego. The paradox is that the more I release the self, the more total I become. I do it for my salvation, here and now. I do it because on a day-to-day basis I can stay out of that pit of selfishness and self-centeredness that isolates me from my fellow man. It makes me feel the truth.

Getting rid of the self-centeredness and isolation that we have is asking yourself when you meet someone not what you think of me, but what can I do for you? Saying those words, "What can I do for you?" can be a total surprise. Kids very often answer, "You can listen to me." Many, many people try to learn how to love. Do the action, and the feeling will follow. Do it, don't try to feel it.

PHILIP: I think that is part of our emotional addiction. Unless we have certain feelings, we aren't going to give anything.

ANNE: Thank God that the feelings don't have to be there in order for it to be effective. There are times when these kids will ask me, "Can I talk to you?" My whole feeling is 'hell no,' I haven't got time to listen to your crap. That's my honest feelings at times, but I sit down and listen to them, and divert my attention from what I really don't want to do to what they are saying to me . . . what are they not able to say to me, what can't they get through? Pretty soon that nasty little ego that didn't want to listen to the crap has gone. The sharing is then going on. I don't very often have that feeling anymore. In the beginning I did. I was so totally self-centered that I honestly didn't know what anybody else had to be self-centered about. That was an honest reaction, an honest feeling I had. I'd hear people talk about self-centeredness and I'd think what have they got to be self-centered about. That's how self-centered I was. And it is embarassing to remember that I was that way at one time. For me, and I know I can only speak for myself, loving and giving; I did this by a conscious decision about seven years ago, and it was strictly pragmatic. Id' go with what works and that's the only thing I know. If it works, I'll do it, if it doesn't, I don't need any part of it. I made a conscious decision to spend the rest of my life in service. It's the only thing that made any sense to me. There is nothing noble, self-sacrificing, nor altruistic about it. I do it and I made the decison because it is the only thing that made me feel good. It is the only thing that made a dull day seem like spring time. It made the whole world brand new; it made colors brighter, it made the air fresher, the wind cleaner, life beautiful. It has nothing to do with anything. It wasn't even spiritual, in the beginning, but it grows to become that. It is simply that devoting my life to service is the best way I know to live. It is the happiest, most beautiful free feeling I've ever had. I made a decison that from that time on I would live my life in service. I am sure there are people that would say, "You're saying the same thing that we are saying, that a life of service is nobility, and religious, and all that." That isn't why I do it. When I get up in the morning and I feel lousy, which occasionally I do, and I got a lot of problems going on inside of me, instead of sitting all day and write about, think about, pray about, meditate about, talk about, figure out and analyze . . . I get off my ass, get dressed, and come into this house and say, "Good morning, everybody. What can I do for you today." Somehow, by the time I go to bed, the problems I woke up with are gone. They are solved. That's a fact and it has happened to me.

PHILIP: I find that the ego itself, not just the existence of it, but its *over* existence is the problem.

ANNE: Is the way I'm explaining it making sense? I have a big ego and I love recognition and all the acolades and the juice I can get. I have an alcoholic ego, and I like all that. Yet, it's very dangerous for me. I cannot allow myself to know why about that. What I do I do because it makes me feel good, and that's why I do it. I am not unselfish, I am not a giving, self-sacrificing person. This is part of why I've said I'v always loved St. Francis, 'cause he wasn't either. He hurt and he found a way out not to hurt. That's the whole message I get from St. Francis's life: the fact that he loved God, yes. I love God, too, but I don't do it for God. I'd love to tell people that I do it for God. I do it in service because it works and because it melts away my insanity.

PHILIP: I really don't think God needs anything done for Him. It's for ourselves that He's created the laws of love, not for Him.

PHILIP: Andrea, haven't you ever run across people who legitimately and honestly communicated the fact that they accepted you and cared about you?

ANDREA: No, not until very recent times. There was a lady, a girl's vice-principal, who is dead now from cancer, who tried to help me. But I felt that she kept betraying me. Everytime I talked to her, she'd go and tell my mother.

PHILIP: What about your husband, lovers, boyfriends? Didn't you get any kind of response from them?

ANDREA: I had one boyfriend that I went with for a long time. I felt like it was him and me against the world. In the end, he betrayed me, too. That's again, "poor little me," but those were the feelings I had. I felt that he betrayed me because he loved his mother more. In the end, his mother won out. I never knew that my mother didn't like him. When I told her that we were engaged, she laughed and said, "Oh, God!" I felt like somebody had just stuck a knife in my gut. I'd never been aware that my mother didn't like him. She'd always treated him very nicely.

PHILIP: What I'm getting at is that for most of your life, at least until you were 25 or the time when you first went to that meeting, you really had not experienced unconditional love?

ANDREA: No, I didn't even know what the meaning of the expression was.

PHILIP: From your experience with alcoholics or young people with potential drinking problems, do you find that to be a general experience?

ANDREA: Yes, I do. We are always graded on our performance. I don't think that fair. That's just the way my mind works; that's just the way I'm recorded inside. I constantly work on that problem. It's just the way I look at it.

PHILIP: In other words, you are aware today that other people can actually have a problem too, and it concerns not being honest with you in terms of their evaluation of you?

ANDREA: Yeah, I think that sometimes. But I think that mostly it's my own lack of self-worth that doesn't believe when people tell me good things about me. I'd rather be screamed and hollered at 'cause I can cope with that. But I cannot cope with somebody being nice to me, especially if I feel I've been a bad girl and I need to be punished.

PHILIP: Do you think that experience, strength, and hope can be somehow communicated in our institutions, in our society?

ANDREA: Sure. Not just by alcoholics and people that are on that program but other human beings that want something better. It's an attraction method in promotion. People watching other people living; the war is over inside. That attracts people that have a war going on if they are tired of it. People that are full of hate don't like me because I'm not full of hate. But they watch a lot, they watch me and they listen to me. Someday they come up and ask, "How did you get there?" I'm tired of hating people." Then I can sit down and talk to them, but I won't try and shove it down their throats.

Sixteen

OUR NEW FOUND HUMOR

At sometime in our life, the life we lived before we found new life in following our spiritual program, incidents occurred where people questioned, "Don't you even have a sense of humor?" And, according to the degree of our ego entanglements and self-will— obsessions, we *didn't* have a sense of humor. On the contrary, certain things—be they sex fulfillment, power or money acquisition—were ultimately important. Life became the serious business of making sure we had what we wanted, that we planned our lives in such a way we could end up having all our ego desires met whenever we felt their urges. Or perhaps we were so negative and unsure of ourselves that fear played the dominant motive in our everyday life. For sure, a sense of humor was rarely or never experienced.

Humor is the state of being centered in our real self so that all those very important things the ego deals with, Reality and Our Self, the world, is not seen as so important. This is when we laugh; seeing things as they really are and enjoying the often wide gulf between what could be and what is. Humor is born in our ability to step out of ourselves and see something "out there," outside our limiting ego. That's why you hear people say, "Don't you see the humor in that?" The "that" they refer to is something not of ourselves, usually. We find, too, that we can do some pretty crazy things. We get so serious as we charge into a situation, something happens that shows us and everybody else how human we really are, and if we are not preoccupied with the ego position of how do I come off to other people, we laugh. To laugh at ourselves, freely and with gusto, is a good indication of reaping the spiritual fruits of our labor.

Our newly developing sense of humor means we feel and express the growing sense of joy we have to know. We no longer worry about other people being sourfaced around us, inhibiting the free expression of those good feelings inside. It now becomes important for us to *be* happy as we get in touch with our inward happiness.

Shakespeare once commented that to those who think, life is a tragedy and to those who feel, life is a comedy. Our feelings now surface more quickly and easily as our once impenetrable ego defenses fall away, replaced by our inner self. Life is fun, we find, as we let the child within us out to play. Emotions grow less distorted, richer, as we approach ourselves and others, the source of our emotional life. All things seem new as we find our sense of humor and freely express ourselves through it.

PHILIP: The program allows you to see your humanness, but in an accepting, nonjudgmental way.

ANDREA: Yeah, I try. There's days when I judge myself and condemn myself. But it isn't like it used to be. It isn't for days on end. It's only maybe a few hours. I talk about it, I don't push it down. I open my mouth and I talk about it and open myself to be able to laugh at myself or have somebody else laugh at me today. I'll die if I don't, and I believe that all people are dying because they can't do that.

PHILIP: Can't do what?

ANDREA:They can't open themselves up, laugh at themselves, see the joke in it. They can't open themselves up to seeing themselves as to who they really are. They can't get down to what's underneath it all. I believe God created us perfect and lacking in nothing. These are just lessons we have to learn to get to that point. The days I love people because they exist lasts longer. I seem to be able to accept people on a better basis than I ever did before, most of the time.

In my second year of sobriety, tney used to call me "Sunshine," and they used to say that she reminds me of a flower who's just put her face to the sun. She's always smiling and laughing. I learned to laugh in the program. I believed God gave me my laugh. That bubbly, warm feeling that just bursts up inside of me . . . and I can't control it nor do I want to. I've had newcomers come up to me and say I've come back just to hear you laugh. I met a man who said that he was sober because he heard me laughing through all the meetings. He never met mc until he was three years sober. He never had the guts to come up and shake my hand. Those are the kinds of things that God worked through me. That is a privilege to me to be used as an instrument because of my past and the way I lived; like an animal. I don't understand that except that it was time.

Seventeen

THE NEW PERSON

Having internalized and practiced the spiritual program we have outlined, we find ourselves gradually assuming the identity and life style of a new person or rather the person we always were but were too busy with our ego-obsession distraction to notice. Let us review again these steps and activities, putting them into our own words, our own understandings of how this applies to me.

1. Through a repeating pattern of frustration, living lives we knew there was more to but found it painfully difficult to discover, trying ways often of the world's doing or the inadequacy of our limiting self-will and "insanity," we came to admit to ourselves our fruitlessness in living a life of strictly our own ego-will, our helplessness in the face of obsessions that dominated us, and emotions and ideas which put us at their harrassing and controlling mercy. We then make a decison and commitment to change, to discover our real self.

2. We're led to the belief in a caring power, available to us to restore us to our proper and true selves and a right relationship with the unfolding of our lives. This power or God which we came to believe in took on the identity that was personal and which happened between us, and no one else.

3. Made a commitment, a decision, to surrender our life, our will over to this caring God as we came to know who He was for us. We sought to renew this surrender, in all the everyday concerns which confront us; understanding that the will of this God can be trusted to realize in our lives our truest and deepest heart aspirations and longing to be ourselves and happy.

4. Confronted ourselves, in the spirit of honesty, openness, willingness, with who we really were, our moral make-up. Called a sin a sin, a feeling a feeling, exactly what it was . . . no cover-ups. Surrendered, lowered the barriers of our defenses like pride and self-righteousness, fear, insecurity, and self-justification.

Allowed our feelings to surface without judging them, condemning them; accepted in a gentle spirit ourselves in spite of whatever we found ourselves to be, and feel . . . forgave ourselves . . . for being just human.

5. Practiced a form of confession by showing God, ourselves, and another trusted understanding human being, just who we were, where we are coming from, our weaknesses, failings, moral deficiencies.

Began seeing ourselves as one human being among other equal human beings, the brotherhood and fellowship of being human. Practiced humility as a kind of openness to change and growth. Forgave others their "trespasses," quickly and forgot them once and for all.

6. Turned to all those weaknesses, inabilities, and character failings which had hindered us from happily and productively living our own life, and realized that our season had come to surrender all these, in a spirit of humility, willingness, and commitment, over to the caring power of God. This "gardener of the spirit" was trusted to gently, and over a period of time, necessitating our patience, removed the hinderances keeping us from living free, in the spirit of love.

7. Recognized the responsibility we have to make right, when we can, and when it is not harmful, the transgressions and wrongs we have done others in the past. Where time, distance, and circumstances prevent this, we did it in our heart.

8. Continued to search ourselves in our every day dealings with people and those internal goings on known only to us, as to our wrongs when we do them, our feelings when we feel them, allowing them to be here and now, quickly acknowledge who we discover ourselves to be and change to our true selves for our own well being.

9. Came to realize that in every problem, crisis, conflict there is an opportunity: to grow, to discover through what those feelings are really saying and deficiencies showing, just who we really are so that reapplying step 6 we can release "old business" and live in a here and now forward direction. We, our feelings, are not to be run from, but worked with, confronted.

10. Practiced as a part of who we are now becoming as full, realized persons, through meditation and prayer, improving our

direct contact with God as we discovered Him to be, and ourselves, too. In meditation we found a safe ground, an inner sanctum, our "hearts" where we could freely discover, accept and work with who we are, enjoy this person we find within, and establish a cooperative spirit from which to go out from and improve and fulfill all the other relationships we enter upon with people.

In prayer we were quick to thankfully accept and acknowledge God's presence, admitting our friend into our and His "home," enjoying God and our friendship; praying to know His will for us and the strength and enthusiasm to carry it out in our lives. Prayed, too, for others, that they come to know and work in the spirit of God in their lives.

11. Entered upon an age of freedom in our lives, releasing the child in us to play, create, enjoy our life and life around us. Began celebrating our self and our life instead of fearing, defending, and avoiding them. Learned how to play and share with others; discovered that we had power over our feelings, a way to go, a program to follow, that we had a choice as to how we were going to feel in *any* situation and with anyone. Began feeling and being aware of the "total support" God gives to us in everything that happens to us. Found freedom in our surrender to love who we are, and the ever present love God is, and offers to us. Allowed ourselves the joy of laughter, humor, especially with ourselves and the 'drama' of our own life. Lingered longer and longer in the here-and-now, seeing the life available to us in the "present" moment, surrendering the guilt of the past and the fear, anxiety, and insecurity of the future. Realized that in the "now" we are *always* with our caring friend God . . . if we choose to be. Made it a regular part of our day to realize the first duty in life, to enjoy oneself, to enjoy living; not renouncing the world, but completing ourselves through it, appreciating it, being in touch with it.

12. Having grown in the spirit, responded, out of gratitude for all we have been given and all we have come to be, with a life of service to ourselves, and our fellow man, realizing that before we can give of ourselves to others, we must be that "self" to give. We attain that self, in a large measure, through unconditional love of self; and serve others in sharing that unconditional love. The spiritual life and our life of service is for us, our true living and the living of others; it is not done for God, but rather through Him.

Service, we discovered, is being who we really are, doing whatever we do with our real self, and enthusiastically. Giving us our dependent or dominating behavior with others, we approached our fellow man as equals having the same heritage, a friend among friends, a person among persons. In this spirit we accepted our respons-i-bility to others for their well being, their person; a responsibility marked by living up to our agreements and commitments towards people, knowing and accepting our limits in making these commitments. Responsibility comes also to mean our ability to respond to another person as we find them to be, in a way that is supportive to their well being. We do this best by getting our own life together.

Took responsibility and ownership of our lives, feelings and decisions, saw that we do in fact fashion the "home" we live in, that no one else is ever to blame. What manure we generate with all the negatives and failings of our lives, we diligently spread around the base of our tree, surrendering the growth process to the spirit of life around and in us.

A shorter verson of these steps, a direct working application, is found in the prayer, "The Our Father." There are other supports and directives available to us in a short, to the point, form such as "Desiderata." Whatever strikes a responsive chord in us, whatever seems to further us along the path of well being, let us respond to it. In psychology, Dr. Murry Banks gives us this short form of mental examination that allows us to diagnose troubled spots and our own mental health temperature:

1. Ask ourselves, "am I happy.." If not, then commit yourself to doing something about it.

2. Do we have zestful living, pursuing new interests, making new friends, expanding our knowledge and awareness of ourselves and the world? Do we enjoy life?

3. Do we have unity and balance? Putting our whole self into what we do, and refraining from placing all our eggs in one basket, one person, relationship, etc.

4. Can we laugh, at ourselves, the world, quickly?

5. Do we have a confidential relationship with someone; someone we trust, and can be ourselves with?

6. Do we see things as they are, and accept them?

7. Do we see people and relationships as ends in themselves, refraining from ulterior motives and just enjoying who and what is in front of us?

8. Can we recognize an opportunity in every crisis? A lesson to be learned?

9. Are we really making contact with God as we understand Him?

10. Do we love, unconditionally, ourselves and others?

The life of the spirit, our total persons, will come to mean for us the realization that we do not have to fill our lives with a constant flow of gratifications, of sensual experiences, desires of body and ego, of time-consuming ventures. This was done in the past, when ego was at the helm, because the peace of our self, and God was yet undiscovered and unacknowledged.

Have you ever sat with some really content people, totally at peace in themselves? Usually older folk. These realized people aren't "doing" all those self-seeking, thinking, scheming, planning, running about, getting it all for me excursions, we of our teens, twenties and thirties are especially noted for. They simply just "are," being themselves. They love, they share, they surrender, and accept and enjoy. They aren't amassing any "thing" or building an empire. They just live in touch with peace and completion of self as we live in and of the spirit. It is our calling as human beings, of we "persons," it is a calling spoken to Adam which led to the Garden of Paradise; the calling of Abraham, Moses, of a "Promised Land," from Christ for the Kingdom of God to be realized in us and for us to know Life, which was to personally know God; it is the calling given us in our own human birth, fashioned and witnessed to by the anguish of our longings and separation of our aloneness. The calling is to life, the joyous participation in the friendship and love of God, seen in the shimmering of stardust on blackened night skies, hopeful dew drops sparkling in the morning dawn, a smile and a laugh worn and heard on our faces, the light in the eyes of those who have truly seen.